Issues in Education

GENERAL EDITOR: PHILIP HILLS

New Perspectives on Disaffection

Other Books in this Series

David Sanders and
Leo B. Hendry

New Perspectives
on Disaffection

CASSELL

Cassell

Wellington House

125 Strand

London WC2R OBB

PO Box 605

Herndon

VA 20172

First published in 1997

British Library Cataloguing-in-Publication Data

A catalogue record for this book is available from the
British Library.

ISBN   0–304–32874–X (hardback)
      0–304–32872–3 (paperback)

Printed and bound in Great Britain by
Biddles Ltd, Guildford and King's Lynn

Contents

Foreword: the purpose of this series

The educational scene is changing rapidly. This change is being caused by a complexity of factors which includes a re-examination of present educational provision against a background of changing social and economic policies, new forms of testing and assessment, a National Curriculum, and local management of schools with more participation by parents.

As the educational process is concerned with every aspect of our lives and of our society both now and for the future, it is of vital importance that all teachers, teachers in training, administrators and educational policy-makers should be aware and informed on current issues in education.

This series of books is thus designed to inform on current issues, to look at emerging ones, and to give an authoritative overview which will be of immense help to all those involved in the education process.

Philip Hills
Cambridge

Preface

Adolescent disaffection and disruption is not a new problem for schools. References have been made to the adverse behaviour of young people and school pupils for centuries. It would appear however that the past decade has seen an escalation of the frequency of disruptive incidents both in and out of schools – at least in terms of media reports. These are made manifest by the steady increase of both fixed-term and permanent exclusions of pupils from their school and the increasing number of delinquents. The level of public concern appears to be mounting probably because the incidents reported are more and more serious and the acts of disruption are committed by younger and younger children. The permanent exclusion of primary school age children, once a rarity, is now relatively commonplace. Even nursery age pupils cannot and do not escape the increased propensity of schools to make use of exclusion as a sanction. How can we account for these changes? Has the way in which parents raise their children deteriorated? Has the regime within schools collapsed? Do changes in society, for example in relation to increasing unemployment, explain the development of more challenging behaviour from young people? Is there a combination of these cause and effect parameters taking place?

This book sets out to explore aspects of disaffection and disruption within community settings and attempts to present new perspectives on the topic. Chapter 1 introduces recent media responses to incidents of disruption and examines the main factors which may account for such behaviour. Chapter

2 examines the response of ten pupils who have been excluded from mainstream education. It considers briefly their
case histories, behavioural record to exclusion and their
views on the quality of the alternative educational provision.
Chapter 3 looks at schools by examining the perceptions,
academic self-concept and self-esteem of a large number of
primary school and secondary school pupils. Chapter 3 also
introduces the theme, which is pursued further in Chapter 4,
that the research looking for the causal factors of pupil
disruption has been flawed by its own simplicity. In the main,
researchers have attempted to identify single causal factors of
pupil disruption: these can be summarized into two groups.
First, those who consider school organization to be the key
context and those who opt for home circumstances. While
home and school are considered, in addition pupils and their
peer group are taken into account, and it is argued that
different responses by pupils to situations and incidents are in
part a contextual product of the reactions of the individual in
accordance with his or her particular character and attributes.
Such reactions may then be reflected in any subsequent
action, and in turn this may be further affected by group
dynamics such as peer pressure. The complexity of the
situation begins to unfold. Chapter 4 also considers the
meaning of the term *disruption* through the eyes of pupils,
teachers and headteachers; and examines the changing pattern
of the permanent exclusion of pupils from a number of
schools. Chapter 5 looks at the role of parents in maintaining
good behavioural standards of their children and parental
perception of home/school partnership. There have been
significant changes in the law on exclusions in England and
Wales and the Department for Education and Employment
has published guidance on this and associated educational
procedures. Chapter 6 looks at these changes and the
background to exclusions, national and authority statistics on
pupil exclusions and educational provision for excluded
pupils. It also draws on the experience of one of the authors
of excluding pupils and of making provision for them, and

includes a post-Elton review of measures and legislation related to disruptive pupils. Chapter 7, the final chapter, looks at the way forward and attempts to answer the following questions amongst others.

1. If levels of disaffection, certainly as measured by school exclusions, are increasing, how does this relate to other parameters of disaffection among young people?

2. What progress has been made in a professional understanding of the dynamics of disaffection and about the provision for those young people involved?

3. What are the 'messages' in our findings to schools and communities, local authorities and national policy-makers?

The book has been informed by the experience of the authors and a study based on 3000 young people in a large Scottish city. The nature and scope of the study is summarized in Appendix A.

1 Adolescence, disaffection and society

Introduction

This chapter looks at the position and transitions of youth in present-day society, and explores some of the psycho-social factors, institutions and contexts which may produce feelings of disaffection and alienation.

The state of British society today has been described as follows:

> The poor are not an unchanging lumpen mass: there is constant churning, with hundreds of thousands regularly falling in and out of the poorest 10 per cent. This has led some to conclude that Britain does not have an underclass – a large cadre of the permanently poor. But this mistakes the nature of the underclass ...
>
> The underclass is not a degree of poverty. It is a type of poverty; it covers those who no longer share the norms and aspirations of the rest of society, who have never known the traditional two-parent family, who have left the official labour force for good, who are prone to abuse drugs and alcohol at the earliest opportunity, who do poorly at school and who are quick to resort to disorderly behaviour and crime. Lack of money is often the least of their problems. Today's deprived youth is likely to be a strapping lad, overweight rather than undernourished, dressed in £100 trainers and designer jeans, wondering whether to watch satellite television or play the latest video game. (Neil, 1995)

The media are quick to point out the negative effects of youth on law and order in society and the confrontational relationship between youth and adult society has often been highlighted, as seen in the following quotation from *The Scotsman*:

> The police is simply the anvil on which youth is beating out its frustration and anger and they seem to be alienated from every conceivable part of society from which they are drawn.
> (West Yorkshire's Assistant Chief Constable quoted by Beale, 1995)

Support for such media views comes from the recent interpretations of academic research: Rutter and Smith (1995) conclude that the post-war rise in youth problems has come about not because of poverty, but because of growing affluence. The authors of the report believe that young people are growing up in a moral vacuum, unable to cope with the freedoms won by youth in the 1960s, and brought up to have expectations that cannot be met. They contend that young people find themselves isolated, inhabiting a 'separate youth culture'.

Cooke (1995) points out that the response to this five-year research from leader writers and commentators is predictable. The blame for this 'lost' generation was placed squarely on parents and their so-called permissiveness during the flower-power era of the 1960s. Nowhere did anyone disagree with the report's central vision of young people as a miserable, stressed-out, self-abusing, inarticulate generation, grown-up precociously and in trouble by their early teens. The report also suggests that with access to fashionable clothes, consumer goods and drink, they are far more likely to suffer from anorexia or alcohol-related problems than their parents were. However, as Cooke wrote:

> Making generalizations about a whole section of society purely on the grounds of age is always going to be fraught with diffi-

culty, and is the case particularly with (Rutter and Smith's) report because it groups together all kinds of problems – from anorexia to burglary – under the term 'psychosocial disorder'.

Perhaps the most sensationally reported nadir of young people's behaviour in society which illustrated views of alienated, disaffected youth was the horrific killing of the toddler, Jamie Bulger, by two pre-adolescent boys in 1993.

But are present-day youth really so terrible? Qvortrup (1994) explains that:

> In the United States most children in prison have not committed crimes, but have been found guilty in status offences, such as running away from home, being incorrigible, truant or sexually precocious. Even within research children are denied the opportunity to speak for themselves, research on childhood has its ingrained expectations. Given the rules that regulate children's behaviour and that determine the borderline for what is deemed a status offence, it seems as if researchers who seriously try to give voice to children or to be serious about their activities in their own right themselves run the risk of violating good scientific behaviour. There is, indeed, a certain logic in this unspoken attitude, namely that to be serious about what children do themselves may be seen as subversive to adults' definition of the rules of the game.

Later he extols adults to 'deal with children as human beings not as human becomings. Children are marginalized. Marginalization may be protective but it may also at the same time be paternalistic.'

In order to clarify the role of youth in society we need to know what adolescence is.

Adolescent transitions in society: developing lifestyles?

What is it like to be an adolescent in present-day Britain? Adolescence, as a time set aside for waiting, developing and maturing and for accomplishing the ill-defined 'rites of passage' between childhood and adult status, is certainly an extended phase of life for today's young people. In the first place, no one is entirely sure when adolescence begins. For some it may be at 13, the first 'teen' year, while for others it may be at the start of secondary school. For those who prefer a physical marker the commencement of puberty is the obvious moment, yet puberty itself is a very complex phenomenon, with different elements – the growth spurt, menarche, and so on – occurring at different times. The picture is further confused by the fact that, during the twentieth century in western industrialized countries, puberty has occurred approximately one month earlier every decade of the century – the so-called secular trend (Coleman and Hendry, 1990). A variety of social pressures and changes in child-rearing practices seem destined to foreshorten that period of life when the young person is truly a child. Maturing to puberty at an earlier age than their parents and grandparents, young people become participants in domestic and global affairs through more open households and the omnipresent media. Thus today's child in some senses at least has entered upon adolescence long before leaving primary school. At the same time oppos-ite forces are in action, compulsory schooling has been extended and the pressures on the workforce to become more highly skilled have put a premium on 'staying on' at school or moving into tertiary education. The delay in acquiring an income is another of the factors which seems to defer the passage to adulthood. The erosion of the traditional roles of the family, the church and the school – institutions originally associated with the socialization of the young – has resulted in a fragmentation of adolescent transitions since various social environments function as independent, sometimes isolated and at times contradictory settings for teenagers. It is this confusion of purpose at the community level and the disaffection which young people may develop towards it, rather than any nationwide rebelliousness towards adult society, which create the possible conflicts of the adolescent identity crisis so frequently cited in the media. The development of a consumer-oriented post-modern society where the young struggle earlier and earlier to gain adult 'accreditation' through fashionable consumer goods and activities, while the old strive to retain the image of youthfulness via similar 'market' products and social contexts, complicates the picture further. As Coleman (1979) points out in emphasizing the teenage period of the life cycle as socially contrived:

> Adolescence is a complex and contradictory stage of development. Adolescent behaviour itself is frequently paradoxical. For example, conformity may go hand-in-hand with rebellion, while spontaneity alternates with sullen reserve.... A spirit of fierce independence is transformed in the space of a few minutes into childish dependence, yet the most difficult teenager may become, almost overnight, a delightful and rewarding companion. Equally confusing are the discrepancies which exist between the images of young people as they are presented in newspapers, or on film or television, and the behaviour of the great majority of adolescents in our society. On the one hand it must seem from the media as if there is no escape from the anger, violence and mindless drifting of the younger generation, yet on the other hand countless hard-working or exam-orientated teenagers are in evidence in every neighbourhood.
>
> (Coleman, 1979)

From a research perspective Coleman (1979) presents a 'focal theory' arguing that the transition between childhood and adulthood cannot be achieved without substantial adjustments of both a psychological and social nature. Nevertheless, despite the amount of overall change experienced, most young people are extremely resilient and appear to cope with adjustments without undue stress.

Coleman's 'focal theory' offers a reason or rationale for this apparent contradiction. In it he proposes that at different ages particular sorts of relationship patterns come into focus, but that no pattern is specific to one age only. Thus the patterns overlap, different issues come into focus at different times, but simply because an issue is not the most prominent feature at a particular age does not mean that it may not be critical for some individuals. Coleman suggests that concern about gender roles and relationships with the opposite sex declines from a peak around 13 years; concerns about acceptance by or rejection from peers are highly important around 15 years; while issues regarding the gaining of independence from parents climb steadily to peak around 16 years and then begin to tail off. Such a theory may provide some insight into the amount of disruption and crisis implicit in adolescence and the relatively successful adaptation among most adolescents. The majority of teenagers cope by dealing with one issue at a time. Adaptation covers a number of years, with the adolescent attempting to solve one issue, then the next. This means that stresses resulting from the need to adapt to new models of behaviour are rarely concentrated all at one time. Those who, for whatever reasons, try to cope with more than one issue at a time are most likely to have problems of adjustment.

> We believe that most young people pace themselves through the adolescent transition. Most of them hold back on one issue, while they are grappling with another. Most sense what they can and cannot cope with, and will, in the real sense of the term, be an active agent in their own development.
>
> (Coleman and Hendry, 1990)

Coffield *et al.* (1986) comment that Coleman's focal model makes no attempt to deal with disadvantages and deprivation. They present a different model derived from their experience of carrying out research in the north-east of England with young people, many of whom were unemployed, all of whom were living at the very periphery of British society. In their model, social class and patriarchy are seen as all-pervading influences which determine to a large extent the options and choices available to young people in this under-privileged section of society. Focal theory has to do with the psychological transitions of adolescence rather than with the economic and social circumstances of the individual. For example, all young people, irrespective of social background, attempt to negotiate increasing independence from their parents. The focal model suggests that it will be easier to handle the parental issue if the young person is not, at the same time, striving for greater acceptance within the peer group.

Coffield *et al.* are right to draw attention to the social circumstances of the individual, for these will obviously contribute in a substantial way to each adolescent's psychological adjustment. Gaining independence from parents has sociological and financial implications – as in unemployment – as well as being a psychological issue. There can be little doubt that in situations of economic hardship it will be more difficult to manage adolescent transitions in a satisfactory manner. Teenagers are less able to cope if at one and the same time they are uncomfortable for example with their bodies, owing to physical changes; with family, owing to changes in the family constellation; with home, because of a move; with school, owing to great discontinuity in the nature of the school environment; or with peers, because of disruption of peer networks and changes in peer expectations and peer evaluation criteria, and because of the emergence of opposite-sex relationships. In recent years social conventions have given adolescents greater self-determination at steadily younger ages and current social expectations for youth are remarkably problematic. As adolescents grow up they are exposed to a larger number and variety of adult role models, both in school and elsewhere, and as our society has become more diverse the number of social roles and choices available to most teenagers increases dramatically. Thus the ways in which young people select among these roles is harder to predict because political and moral values have become more diffuse as we have moved to a pluralistic post-modern society.

Since young people are reared in a social milieu which is quite different from that of their parents individuals have to 'carry' with them into society the stamp of their own particular family lifestyle, yet tailored to suit young people's contemporary social requirements. During adolescence young people are exposed to new social situations and need different social skills than those required in earlier childhood. The shift from childhood to adolescence is marked by change in many aspects of social life (Damon, 1983). During adolescence peer relations become more intense and extensive, family relations are altered, and the adolescent begins to encounter many new demands, expectations and social contexts. Adolescents may begin dating, working with others in a part-time job, or spending time with peers without adult supervision. Several developmental changes serve to alter the manner in which adolescents interact with others. These include more advanced cognitive, verbal and reasoning abilities and the changes associated with puberty. Importantly, the transition to adulthood contains within it the 'taking on' of adult-like behaviours. There are several aspects of adult society both legal and illegal which young people 'tune into' as emergent consumers – smoking, drinking, drugs, under-age sex, joyriding and general disruptive behaviour around mass spectacles such as pop concerts and soccer matches. Many of these activities involve the adolescent in risk or risky behaviours. The need to assert and confirm a separate identity is clearly evident amongst young people. Here the peer group often acts to regulate expressive behaviour. Accordingly, it becomes difficult for adolescents to resist what Brake (1985) calls a 'quasi-delinquent style' in the hiatus between childhood and adulthood, given the absence of clear social roles for them to perform. For example, the machismo associated with male working-class youth subculture (e.g. 'joy-riding', aggressive behaviour) represents a group response to the objective realities facing young people in a world of unemployment, low pay and low self-esteem (see Murdock and Phelps, 1973; Willis, 1977).

Lifestyles express a collective identity for group members and lifestyles differentiate the group. The most important point, however, is that lifestyle sets a particular group apart from others. In contemporary society dominant ideas about work, health and leisure are the backdrop against which many lifestyles are enacted. For example, there has been much recent interest in lifestyles in relation to health and in particular health promotion (Aaro *et al.*, 1986). In the context of health Wenzel (1982) defined the lifestyle of an individual as 'the entirety of normative orientation and behaviour patterns which are developed through the processes of socialization'. Abel and McQueen (1992) operationalize lifestyle in terms of a complex patterning of three basic elements; '**behaviours**', '**orientations**' and '**resources**'. The first two of these are elements of choice or conduct. The third is related to the structural factor of 'life chances'. These basic dimensions interact to form an individual's way of life. Structural constraints at a societal level (e.g. Giddens, 1984) affect these interactions amongst behaviours, orientations and resources. Hence the interplay of structurally rooted 'life chances' and individual 'life conduct' results in the emergence of lifestyles as collective phenomena which allow for social differentiation both within and between groups. Lifestyles can be regarded as the product of interactions amongst a complex network of interdependent factors. They are the means through which individuals assert and confirm their position within society. Understanding adolescent lifestyles consists not only of gauging young people's behaviour but also includes understanding their attitudes, values and orientations in relation to the material and cultural resources available to them.

The transitions of adolescence may be broadly similar for the majority of young people but the nature of the pathways

9

followed through these transitions may vary from individual to individual, and from sub-cultural group to group. In taking account of some of these 'pathways' and variabilities in development Hendry *et al.*'s (1993b) lifestyle analysis points out not only clear-cut social class and gender differences by mid- to late adolescence but also important lifestyle variations within – and, less significantly, across – social class boundaries. Young people's lifestyles appeared to be clearly differentiated across a range of psycho-social factors. These factors come from within the individual and from the various contexts young people find themselves in and can be seen as an interaction of self-perceptions, motivations, meanings and saliences which adolescents put upon various social and leisure activities; ecological influences such as living conditions; parenting styles and family composition; school; peer groups and facets of wider cultural effects such as the mass media. These impinge on various social aspects of living in modern society such as being unemployed or moving towards higher education or being involved in risk-taking behaviours such as drug misuse. Based on Hendry *et al.*'s (1993) findings lifestyle development between mid-adolescence and late adolescence would appear to be strongly linked to young people's educational–occupational trajectories and to their 'life chances'. However, it is important to note that there were a variety of working-class lifestyles; and a variety of middle-class lifestyles; and that a few adolescent lifestyles 'cut across' class boundaries. Those that did were typically associated with youth-oriented cultures. Thus, a variety of distinctive adolescent lifestyles were apparent. However, defined, key components of lifestyles would seem to be: characteristics of the person; characteristics of his/her ecology; and links to wider cultural/social institutions and values.

The dominant values operating in today's society, consumerism, the state of the family, the training and employment landscape facing adolescents, rising homelessness, drugs, the threat of AIDS, crime and lawlessness bring into focus reflections of the adult world that young people face in their journey across adolescence. Over the past fifteen years we have seen the development of consumerism and the establishment of the primacy of the market-place, together with its influence on the occupational and social aspects of young people's development. This has occurred at a time when the behaviour of young people has come under increasing scrutiny by policy-makers and when, despite young people's rights being protected in law, there has been an erosion of autonomy and a depletion of rights, particularly those related to independence which is one of the hallmarks young people seek in approaching adulthood. Frost and Stein (1989) argue, however, that though youth is a disadvantaging factor in present-day society, poverty, race, and gender may be as important structurally in determining life chances. Thus, we may need to remember clearly that the transitions from youth to adulthood are complex, fragmented and influenced by systematic social inequalities, and that youth is not necessarily a homogeneous group within society.

Risk behaviours

Though risk-taking has been one of the attributes of youth since adolescence became recognized as a distinctive period of the lifespan, the concept remains ill-defined. Are young people at risk because they pursue different courses of action to adults? Or do they pursue very similar courses of action but are more vulnerable because they lack the learned potential to resolve situations to their advantage? From where does this supposed predilection for risk-taking derive? Is it part of the psychological make-up of youth – a thrill-seeking stage in a developmental transition – a necessary rite of passage *en route* to the acquisition of adult skills and self-esteem? Or is it a consequence of a social or cultural urge by adults to marginalize youth because their transition from controllable child to controlled adult is a threat to the stability of the community?

Before we begin to discuss risk behaviours in any detail, it is important that we understand that there are several kinds of risk behaviours and that these produce very different responses from and effects in individuals.

First, **thrill-seeking behaviours.** These are behaviours which test the limits of one's own capacities. In these activities there is total concentration, little or no self-consciousness and a sense of self-transcendency resulting from a merging of consciousness with action (Csikszentmihalyi, 1975). These flow experiences, as Csikszentmihalyi names them, offer experiences which are sufficiently challenging to engage a full measure of the individual's skills but are not so demanding as to be anxiety provoking. Activities which provide clear feedback are most likely to be flow producing but the matching of challenges and skills is critical. If challenges are greater than skills, anxiety results, while a lack of challenge in relation to available skills is likely to be experienced as boredom. What is certain is that flow provides a highly vivid climatic set of experiences. Descriptions of the feeling of flow indicate an experience that is totally satisfying beyond a sense of having fun. Enjoyment of the feeling may be akin to a peak experience in quality but its value is considered to be in its promotion of psychological growth.

> Like a built-in thermostat that indicates whether we are operating at full capacity at the leading edge of growth
>
> (Csikszentmihalyi and Larson, 1984)

Such testing, thrill-seeking behaviour can be seen in children as well as in adolescents, in activities such as skiing or diving or provoking adults. But as children they are regarded as non-responsible, lacking in resources (such as money or vehicles and non-supervised time). Thus the thrill-seeking is not regarded as particularly problematic. Beyond adolescence people are aware to a greater extent of their limits and do not engage in so much thrill-seeking behaviour. It is important to stress, however, that some adults still do pursue thrills and excitement. So thrill-seeking is not a feature of youth alone. Adults have more resources to accomplish such behaviours (e.g. going on climbing expeditions or on safari holidays) and further their behaviour as adults is much more accepted by society. Nevertheless, as in the tragedy of the young woman climber, the mother of two children, killed in 1995 in an avalanche on K2, this testing to the limits can have serious results.

Secondly, **risk behaviour in response to group pressures.** It is important to stress here that much of what is called risk-taking behaviour is a male group response. In order to find a place in the peer group, males often believe they have to demonstrate machismo qualities. It is clear that very little risk or risky behaviours are carried out alone. Thus they are carried out in order to demonstrate behaviours to the group so that the individual can find a place in the group hierarchy. Once that is achieved, it is less necessary to continue such behaviours. This may be why adults do not engage so often in group risk behaviours as they have symbolic means of demonstrating their status such as titles, the wearing of expensive clothes or possessing an expensive sports car. This kind of behaviour is also something that young people share with adults but their opportunities to transfer peer-induced risk behaviour to symbols are much more limited.

Thirdly, there are **irresponsible behaviours.** Taking risks, **not** for the thrill but in spite of the risk in order to achieve other goals. Examples such as smoking and unprotected sex make clear this form of behaviour. In connection with this definition, ideas of 'the perceived invulnerability of youth' (Plant and Plant, 1992) make sense: if one believes nothing can happen, where is the thrill? Then the activity is carried out (subjectively) not as a risk behaviour. Such irresponsible behaviours demonstrate the inability of individuals to see long-term consequences or, if these are apparent, to be unable to abstain from them because of the short-term advantages perceived to be gained. It is important at this point to raise the question of why similar behaviours are more accepted in adults and not seen as problematic as these behaviours are in youth. Partly it may be due to the higher vulnerability of youth but partly it may also be that adults are more aware that such behaviour can lead to loss of societal privileges. Additionally, we may at this point be discussing a kind of media campaign against adolescents because adults do, by no means, act more responsibly at all times. For instance, travelling to Thailand to have unprotected sex is carried out by individuals far beyond their teenage years. Or we can consider those adults who eat unhealthily. Where the media is involved, it seems almost ridiculous and unfair that advertising for peace education or environmental protection is directed to youth – as if it were adolescents who started wars or polluted the environment!

Fourthly, there are **damaging behaviours** not necessarily seen as a problem by adult society but nevertheless harming to the young. Examples here are over-heavy sports training at too young an age; academic stress and overachievement; using an unhealthy diet or taking anabolic steroids or chemical preparations in slimming or body-building.

Fifthly, '**criminal behaviour**'. What is criminal is defined by adults. Yet seen as damage done to society, adults can be more destructive than young people. For instance, what is joyriding against speculating away millions of investors' money or promoting tobacco use? In this 'at risk' scenario, young people as a population are often described as a 'problem' and the demands on education are around socializing them more efficiently into the norms and mores of adult society. As Hurrelman and Losel (1990) suggest, personal behaviours in adolescence can contribute to morbidity and mortality: smoking, heavy drinking, using illegal drugs, precocious and unprotected sexual activity, no regular participation in sports and exercise, traffic accidents, violent, aggressive and delinquent activities 'indicate that the image of "healthy adolescence" is inaccurate'.

One cannot discount the possibility that crime and delinquency in our society are in some measure the cost of certain kinds of social development. It has been argued that the predominant ethic of our society is acquisitiveness and desire for success. But not everyone can be rich or successful legitimately. Several writers have pointed out that the values underlying juvenile delinquency may be far less deviant than is commonly assumed. Some crimes reflect media images of the age and gender of the perpetrators. Much media attention has focused recently on the fad of joyriding – stealing cars and performing stunt tricks in them, even though relatively few young people are actually involved in this. More threateningly perhaps from an adult perspective – as a recurring theme from the 1960s, the early and mid-1980s, and the early 1990s – several inner city areas of Britain witnessed events variously described as riots, disturbances and uprisings. While such behaviour is partly thrill-seeking and partly the influence of group pressure, young people are also reacting against adultist and social class suppression (e.g. Brake, 1985). The relationship between social deprivation, status frustration and race has moved juvenile crime to centre stage in policy matters:

> With the observation that there are gross differences in the rate of delinquency by class, by ethnic affiliation, by urban or rural residence, by region and perhaps by nation, from these gross differences the sociologist infers that something beyond the intimacy of family surroundings is operative in the emergence of delinquency patterns, something in the cultural and social atmosphere apparent in sections of society.
>
> (Wadsworth, 1979)

A number of qualifying points need to be made here: first, that the 'criminalizing' of certain forms of activity by adults may enhance their attraction and appeal for some young people, particularly if the activity is associated with media 'hype'; secondly, that labelling occurs when the same kind of activity is criminalized for some (e.g. soccer fans travelling to another town) and categorized as 'high spirits' in others (e.g. misbehaviour on a rugby club outing). This labelling process also applies within the criminal system – often with a social class bias – in decisions about young people's appearance before children's panels or local magistrates and subsequent sentencing (Hendry and Shucksmith, 1994). Additionally, within the justice system young men and young women are often treated differently: young women are less likely to be brought to court, but if they are then they will be treated more harshly, and will be more likely to receive a custodial sentence.

Hence the adolescent years are a period when great adjustments have to be made by young people to changes both within themselves and in society and in relation to the expectations which society places on them. Many young people make the transition to adulthood with relative ease but some are handicapped by economic and structural forces which make their passage to a worthwhile adult status very difficult. Others have the misfortune to have to cope with too many challenges to their self-esteem and identity at one time. For some young people in these positions antisocial behaviour or self-destructive behaviour can be the consequence of their need to find either status or solace. Yet this deficit theory is not sufficient in itself to explain the attraction of taking risks, and an understanding of the very positive attraction of thrilling and dangerous behaviours for some adolescents and the promises and denials held out to youth by the various sectors of adult society are important to understand.

With regard to behaviours we need to ask why young people take risks of the various kinds defined above. Certainly there is a developmental factor in such behaviours. Many young people in their teenage years seek out thrills, excitement and risks as earnestly as they did in childhood, perhaps to escape from a drab existence, to exert some control over their own lives, or to achieve something. Once we start to make the journey into adulthood there are fewer legitimate venues for risk taking and the ones left open to us as adults often bear serious consequences: for instance, those who see juvenile crimes only as a protest of the underprivileged deny the real thrill that such delinquent activities can inspire.

Sport in general can be a positive experience for certain adolescents, but as Csikszentmihalyi and Larson (1984) point out, so too can socializing, eating and travelling in a car. So too, we could add, can stealing and driving away someone else's car, or injecting drugs. Thus, various psycho-social activities can (potentially) provide therapeutic effects. Yet little is known of the properties, contexts and motivations which generate emotional effects for young people in present-day society. Young people who organize themselves for the purpose of playing games are well regarded for their potential to create developmentally important experiences in the process (Devereux, 1976). But games are certainly not the only medium around which children and adolescents will organize (nor are they particularly the best ones considering their vulnerability to being co-opted by the forces of organized sport). The possibility that illegal or deviant activities (for example, drug use) may be among the more attractive alternatives for youth should only be regarded as a challenge to the purpose of identifying and developing the wealth of abilities and interests which adolescents possess. Though the majority of young people are hard-working, law abiding and conventional, some adolescents exhibit rebellion both in their self-presentation and in their behaviour. In relation to social problems in general a number of studies have emphasized the role of identity processes in determining behaviour (Emler, 1984). The desire to identify with a peer group, especially in mid-adolescence (Coleman and Hendry, 1990), requires adherence to particular types of behaviour and role performance which imposes a group conformity even when anti-social actions may result.

But it also appears that the quest for excitement and violence is symbolic in the sense that young people 'use' these behaviours to identify, however misguidedly, with adult patterns of behaviour. Research has focused, especially, on drug and alcohol use, cigarette smoking, sexual behaviour and delinquency. Most of these behaviours would not be alarming if seen in adults but are perceived as being inappropriate for young people in the process of growing up. Silbereisen *et al.* (1987) propose that a number of so-called anti-social activities are in fact purposive, self-regulating and aimed at coping with aspects of adolescent development. They can play a constructive developmental role at least over a short term. Early sexual activity and early child-bearing may have similar functions in providing a positive role and goal in young people's lives (Petersen *et al.*, 1987). While such behaviour is symbolic (i.e. these activities are usually engaged in because of a desire to create a self-image of maturity or as a perceived means of attaining attractiveness and sociability) they nevertheless can put adolescents at risk. Like adults, teenagers typically adopt behaviours in the belief that they will help achieve some desired end such as giving pleasure or gaining peer acceptance. In doing so they are likely to ignore or discount evidence that particular behaviours may pose a potential threat to them.

Many of the explanations regarding adolescent risk behaviour thus rest on accounts of the development of the individual. Both Irwin (1989) and Jack (1989), for instance, consider that risk-taking is a normal transitional behaviour during adolescence. Indeed risk-taking is seen as fulfilling developmental needs related to autonomy and the need for mastery and individuation (Irwin and Millstein, 1986). In practice, what those who work with young people observe is a perceived invulnerability (or, as Plant and Plant (1992) would have it, an imagined vulnerability) to danger, whether this is in relation to road traffic accidents, or to the consequences of over-indulgence in alcohol, smoking and so on. Elkind (1985) characterizes this as the 'Personal Fable' and has described its role in assuring adolescents that they are special and unique. In other words, it allows young people to enhance their self-esteem by believing that they can perform risky acts without experiencing the negative sequelae.

Children and young people, like adults, experience inequality according to social class, gender, ethnicity and disability but their experience cannot be fully understood unless the lack of empowerment associated with their age is also recognized (Frost and Stein, 1989). This inability to view things from young people's perspective often provokes their alienation from adult society. At the same time, adult society is concerned with young people's apparent alienation from the perceived traditional values of this society made visible by those (often a minority of teenagers) engaged in joyriding, under-age sexual relations, vandalism, 'breaking and entering', and drug abuse (Davis, 1990). Jessor (1991), however, points to the fact that many of the apparently organized patterns of adolescent risk behaviour stem from the social ecology of adolescent life rather than from purely psychological sources. Thus this ecology provides socially organized opportunities to learn risk behaviours together and normative expectations that they be performed together. Risk-taking, according to Jessor, is by definition, entwined with lifestyle.

Hence it is clear that risk behaviours take many forms and that though young people are visible in society as participants in various forms of risk behaviours, in many cases they share similar reasons for involvement with adults. The main differences being that young people's reactions are sometimes less skilfully yet more forcefully put into operation and that they have not had the experience of adults in reacting in more socially approved ways. Nevertheless risk behaviours in adolescents are developmental and are part of the learning procedures of growing towards adulthood. In addition they provide or have within them certain qualities that appear to be necessary and conducive to the individual's mental well-being. The fact that they are symbolic while at the same time being exciting and thrilling makes them part of the socialization process and indeed reflects either positively or negatively some of the wider values inherent in our society.

Possible causes and contexts of alienation, disruption and risk taking

Broadly speaking incidents of misbehaviour can be classified into two groups. First, the very serious incident which is relatively uncommon but attracts the most interest from the media and second, the minor but very frequently occurring acts of disruption which can be more harmful in the long term and more stressful for adults such as teachers to deal with (Wheldall and Merrett, 1984). If precise definitions of disruption are difficult, if not impossible, to arrive at then it is even more difficult to assess the line or the boundary through which a young person passes from one side to being regarded as disruptive on the other. Assessment in this crucial area is crude and very subjective and yet it can be argued that identification of this boundary is vital if early recognition of and provision for a young person's needs are going to be possible. Experience suggests that for many children and young people, the signs of disaffection are not apparent until a long period of incubation of the 'condition' has elapsed.

Clearly the way in which the term disruptive is applied varies and it is perhaps appropriate to continue discussion on disaffected adolescents and disruption in this first chapter by referring to Topping (1983), who argues that like intelligence, disruptive is a semantically loose vernacular word and serves its function best by so remaining, providing this is understood, while Lawrence *et al.* (1981) advocated the use of a broad definition, suggesting that it is:

> more specific than descriptions such as naughty... less clinical than maladjusted and less criminological than delinquent.

However, more generally disruption may be defined as:

> any behaviour that in the long run puts the individual adolescent at risk physiologically, mentally (psychologically) or socially

within the context of power relationships between adolescents and adults.

It is important to add, at this point, that disruption is defined for young people by others. For example, a pupil chewing gum in a classroom is carrying out a perfectly normal, and 'neutral', activity, until a teacher declares it as breaking behavioural (school) norms and therefore 'disruptive', or a group of teenage boys chatting at a street corner are engaged in an everyday social action until a policeman decides they are obstructing the footpath or are (somehow) a threat to passers-by and moves them on for being 'disruptive'. Thus the definition as imposed by others always contains within it the suggestion of threat or 'social handicap'.

A variety of possible causes and contexts can be proposed in relation to disruption, alienation and risk-taking in adolescence. Certain of these 'key' aspects are now considered, and these are: self development; marginalization of youth; youth's status in society; the family; schools and schooling; and the transition to the adult world.

Self-development

The adolescents' sense of competence and ultimately their self-concept and future personal identity depend on how well expectations are accepted and processed into personal lifestyles at this stage of development. If these behaviour patterns fit the requirements of roles encountered at school, at work, in relationships, and in community life generally, then the outcome is satisfactory. Alternatively, if they fail to gain structure in their personal identity, confusion and conflict may result, as Erikson (1968) has proposed. He suggests that there are eight psycho-social crises extending through the individual's lifespan which establish stages in the development of personal maturity. He believes that the search for identity becomes especially acute during adolescence as a result of rapid changes in the biological, social and psychological aspects of the individual, and because of the necessity for occupational decisions to be made, ideals to be accepted or rejected and sexual and friendship choices to be determined.

The sources for the development of self-esteem rest primarily in reflected appraisals and social comparisons. Young people compare their competencies with those of their peers in order to discern their level of worth. A cross-sectional survey of nearly 2000 schoolchildren by Simmons *et al.* (1973) identifies early adolescents as experiencing the most difficulty with self-esteem. On the basis of this study they argued that the ages between 13 and 17 years are associated with sharp increases in anti-social behaviour, suicide attempts, drug and alcohol abuse, eating disorders and depression. Entry to a new period in the life-course may challenge the self-image, particularly individuals' self-evaluations, as they attempt new tasks in which they can succeed or fail, as they alter their values and the areas which are important for overall self-esteem and as they confront new significant others against whom they rate themselves and about whose judgements they care. Indeed Kaplan (1980) states that children turn to delinquency after a history of devaluing social feedback which has produced negative self-esteem. Delinquent behaviour is then adopted because it inflates self-esteem through behavioural rewards and psychological defences which allow the delinquent to reject general social feedback and to raise his or her self-perceptions. As a general principle, Kaplan asserts that individuals who have experienced fewer devaluing experiences will require less self-enhancement. Related to the specifics of self-enhancement, Kaplan proposes three psychological defences: denial or personal responsibility for actions, reduction of aspirations and the disguising of deficiencies. Thus, according to Kaplan delinquents employ psychological defences to enhance self-esteem and to retain endorsement of socially accepted values. Denial and rejection of general social feedback and incongruencies between behaviour and self-perceptions appear to be the primary defences and such claims are supported in a study by Zieman and Benson (1983).

An ecology of youth: marginalization?

It can be suggested that the individual is shaped by the context (geographical, historical, social and political) in which he/she finds him/herself and in turn the individual affects changes in that environment. Young people therefore are subject to the influences of significant others in their lives while at the same time the young people actively develop and sustain relationships with these individuals, be they parents, peers or adults outside the family such as teachers, youth leaders, sports coaches and so on. One attempt to describe the context of adolescents' experiences and to provide insights into the joint effects of environment and biological change – a study of human ecology – was carried out by Montemayor and Van Komen (1986). They claim their work demonstrates extensive age-segregation in American society, with adults and young people pursuing their own separate and independent lives. They state too, that, in general, the frequency of interactions with adults decreases as adolescents became older. This is mirrored by Marsland's (1987) view of British society.

> The crucial social meaning of youth is withdrawal from adult control and influence compared with childhood. Peer groups are the milieu into which young people withdraw. Time and space is handed over to young people to work out for themselves in auto-socialization the development problems of self and identity which cannot be handled by the simple direct socialization appropriate to childhood.
>
> (Marsland, 1987)

Blyth *et al.* (1982), however, argue against an age-segregation hypothesis. In their investigation many significant adults are listed, indicating adolescents' regard for and need of adults in their lives and that adult-adolescent relationships are indeed seen as important by adolescents.

Youth in society

Earlier 'classical' theories of adolescence have established certain trends, emphases and biases which seem still to be reflected in modern views about the transition from childhood to adulthood. In an interesting and wide-ranging book on adolescence, Lloyd (1985) outlines a number of key historical theories which have helped to create public 'images' of adolescence. Amongst these significant theories, Stanley Hall's view of adolescence as being a time of 'storm and stress' still maintains currency in the public's mind; as do Freud's ideas that human behaviour is motivated by unconscious psycho-sexual forces. The work of Ruth Benedict and Margaret Mead in primitive societies has also brought to public attention the differing effects of cultural forces on young people's development. Davis (1990) shows, by tracing historically the general public 'images' of adolescents in society, that themes of rebellion, moodiness and 'angst', delinquency, 'sinfulness', energy, excitement and idealistic views of future society have been retained in adults' consciousness, and reinforced by the mass media, in creating stereotypic pictures of youth in Britain today.

Davis traces the history of notions like 'youth as national (economic) asset', 'youth as minority stereotype' (positive as well as negative) and 'youth as a litmus test' (of the good and ills of the society). He demonstrates how these, though waxing and waning, have all (sometimes simultaneously) been key themes in the history of the concept. And he also illustrates how, alongside all this, and especially from the 1960s onwards, a 'youth culturalization' of mainstream adult culture has taken place. What makes this even more paradoxical is Davis's central theme: 'youth as continuity'. For he, like many others before him, provides ample evidence that, far from being revolutionary or even passively subversive, over many generations young people have been deeply committed to the basic values and institutions of their society. The problem (especially for them) has been that adult power-holders have needed to construct images and to accumulate 'data' which 'prove' the opposite in order to justify their requirement for controlling youth and to justify their highly oppressive responses to youth.

In this way Davis (1990) reminds us that youth can be viewed as the 'litmus paper' for the 'condition of society'. In conjunction with this, despite overt attempts to convince us that to adult society young people's interests are paramount (as in the passing of the Children Act (HMSO, 1989)) young people are not seen within the welfare system as having the potential to exercise considered judgement or autonomy. Thus 16-year-olds in the UK, whatever their circumstances, have no entitlement to social security support. It is envisaged that forcing families to assume responsibility for young people into their twenties will both transform 'family values' and relieve the state of the responsibility for social policy in relation to the young (Hendry *et al.*, 1995). Brannen *et al.* (1994) also found occasion in their work to dredge up the problem of social control of young people, and have documented the extent to which youth is asked to 'carry the can' when all is not well with the economic or moral well-being of the nation. We live in such times currently, and parents are continually being exhorted to take more responsibility for the actions and attitudes of their offspring. This is difficult for both parents and teenage offspring to negotiate when there are also these countervailing forces suggesting that young people should be empowered and made autonomous:

The current emphasis upon parental responsibility in controlling young people's anti-social behaviour occurs in an economic climate in which young people's future, in terms of job opportunities, is bleak. It is also a moral climate in which the rights and responsibilities of community and citizenship have been ousted in favour of the values of the marketplace. Parents are being required to fill an economic and moral vacuum.

(Brannen *et al*, 1994)

Adolescents and families

In Britain nearly 50 per cent of marriages end in divorce, while in America around 45 per cent of young people are no longer living with their fathers by the time they reach 18 years of age. As Seccombe's (1993) history of working-class families shows, this situation is very different from 70, 50 or even 25 years ago. Family units have always existed though their size, shape and form have been ceaselessly altering (Adams and Gullotta, 1983). The regular stable unit of 50 or 25 years ago was the passing product of special political and economic circumstances: full male employment, a state social security system, trade union power which secured working men pay packets adequate to support all their dependents, growing prosperity, bourgeois ideals and values percolating through the various class strata of society, and the universal availability of contraception. Thus Seccombe's study shows that changing family patterns are essentially responses to wider economic change. Households have never been capsules, hermetically sealed from socio-economic pressures. Families mutate symbiotically with economic demands and prospects. Like everything else, they have to adjust to market opportunities. The values of Seccombe's book lies in showing it would be ridiculous to hanker after yesterday's model family in the circumstances of today's – or tomorrow's – marketplace. The fluctuations and fissures of the economic scene may well be reflected in the various types of households visible in today's social landscape.

Social shifts have created new constraints, experiences and opportunities for adolescents, in a context where even well-established social institutions can be subject to change. The family unit is one example of how a social institution has developed a variety of models in recent times. The nuclear family is now juxtaposed with 'reconstituted' families, shared custody arrangements and single-parent homes. As Kreppner and Lerner (1989) put it:

> The study of human development has evolved beyond the point of emphasizing the need to study reciprocal relations between the developing person and the family ... now the family is seen as one link amongst other key concepts – the peer group, the school and the work place.

Looking at the social situation and the condition of family life in Britain from Seccombe's perspective it is important to note that any consideration of young people's lives within modern Britain must first acknowledge the structure of British society itself. Despite dramatic structural shifts in recent years, there is still a profound linkage between social class background and the life chances of young people. Hendry *et al.*'s (1993a) findings from a seven-year longitudinal study suggest that the majority of young people may be regarded as 'conventional' while a substantial minority of young people could be described as 'disaffected'. This is bound up with young people's home circumstances and the socio-economic status of the family. Young people from 'conventional' groups were more likely to come from 'non-manual' home backgrounds, for example, and 'disaffected' young people were more likely to come from 'manual' households. Further, findings suggested that youth 'type' is not only associated with social class background, but it is also linked to young people's educational and occupational trajectories and to their subsequent labour market position in later adolescence. Young people from the 'disaffected' group were much more likely to leave school with fewer educational qualifications and to be economically inactive in later adolescence. With regard to the connections between social class background and aspects of lifestyle associated with health, it appeared that an 'unhealthy' lifestyle was less likely to be associated with young people from the 'conventional' group, while an 'unhealthy' lifestyle was most likely to be found in young people from the 'disaffected' group. With regard to smoking behaviour, 'conventional' youth were much less likely to report that they smoked regularly; and with regard to drinking, 'disaffected' youth were more likely to report drinking regularly. Further, it was notable that elements such as 'disaffection' with school, affiliation to the peer group, and the rejection of adult values were closely related to various aspects of youth cultures. Similarly, Brake (1985) has argued that the formation of youth cultures has a structural, and particularly a social class basis in pupil's expressions of personal and social identities.

Economic and social changes portend a number of paradoxes for young people, since the present position of youth in society has been structured by government policy. Until the past decade the majority of young people travelled along well-signposted career trajectories (Roberts, 1984). Their home background and educational streams enabled them to anticipate their initial occupations, and, realistically, the types of adult employment to which these early jobs would lead. With the emergence of youth unemployment in recent years the transition to adult society has become more problematic (Wallace, 1986). What is clear is that by the late 1980s – by comparison with previous generations of young people – entry routes to the labour market had become both diverse and complex (Roberts and Parsell, 1990). As Coffield *et al.* (1986) have pointed out, leaving school, starting work and associating with adults are often judged by young people as central to the process of growing up. For some adolescents there is a clear conflict between the values of schooling and the social and economic 'signs and symbols' of approaching adulthood. Such 'pathways' to the adult world of work – or its denial in unemployment – have created social divisions, and with it an underclass of young people who feel alienated and worthless as the malignancy of unemployment erodes their confidence and stability.

Hendry (1993) suggests that the changing social scene has, in some senses, 'de-skilled parents' simply because they no longer have direct experience themselves of some of the social contexts and behaviours that their adolescent children are experiencing and therefore feel unable to give, and lack confidence in giving, advice to their family beyond general views regarding the legality of particular behaviours and about personal moral values. With regard to parenting styles and their influence, Hendry *et al.* (1993b) show their importance to adolescents' physical and mental health and to the development of lifestyle. They argue that one particular parenting style seemed to have important effects even after a number of years, including an influence on mental health. The neglectful family stood out as quite distinct from other types. Adolescents growing up within this parenting style were more likely to spend more time with the peer group than other adolescents and they had very negative attitudes to school as well as to the family itself. They were also more likely to feel peer pressure to drink and smoke and to regard theft and vandalism as justified within certain circumstances. Although they spent long periods with friends they did not regard themselves as easy to get along with and they were more likely to report psychological stress. The were also likely to have low self-esteem.

Schools and schooling

At this point it is important to consider the role of schools as one of the crucial socializing institutions for young people in our society. The Elton Committee (1989) talks of a growing perception of schools as increasingly anarchic and disorderly:

> The popular press has created the impression of a rising tide of violence and hooliganism, high levels of truancy, abuse of drugs and alcohol among the young and a decrease in respect for authority in school and out.

However, Docking (1980) argues that discipline is in itself an integral part of teaching and cannot be neatly separated from the teacher's main purpose of teaching pupils to learn. The ideological aspect of this function is spelled out forcibly by Furlong (1991):

> When we as teachers use our power in school, when our actions become part of the political structure for the pupils that we teach, then what we are trying to do with our power is to change our pupils in very fundamental ways. Through our power we attempt to try to get children to accept certain values, to aspire to certain futures for themselves. Education structures are used not just to **impose** certain sorts of behaviour but to **construct** young people in particular ways. We do not use our power simply to force children to act in these ways. Rather we insist that they come to see themselves and organize their lives in these ways.

Oldman (1994) also comments on this issue:

> ... let us take the paradigm of teachers and pupils. Where, it seems to me, that teachers can be said to exploit children's labour in a compulsory school setting is through the maintenance of an essentially undemocratic organization of classroom activity ... one never quite loses the feeling that the alienation in most children's experience of school (characterized by the subjective feelings of boredom and irrelevance, and by occasional attempts at subversion) is generated by those organizational features of schooling that the staff require to rationalize and justify the salaries they take from the system ...

These are the features that create manageable working conditions for teachers and are not necessarily the optimal conditions for the self-capitalization of children.

If we look at the school situation in Britain evidence is available about young people being 'shaped in the image of their teachers'. As Henry (1966) wrote, 'School metamorphoses the child ... then proceeds to minister to the self it has created.' In this process various elements of the school system can combine to differentiate pupils in terms of their attitudes toward teachers, their self-images, and their scholastic success.

The labels which teachers may use in 'getting to know' their pupils are outlined by Hargreaves *et al.* (1975): (a) appearance; (b) conformity (or its opposite) to discipline role aspects; (c) conformity (or its opposite) to academic role aspects; (d) likeability; and (e) peer-group relations. It can be argued that conformity, attractiveness, skill, and even 'hidden' sex roles could be major factors in the teacher's expectancies of pupils' performance. The 'hidden curriculum' has been described as the unplanned and often unrecognized values taught and learned through the process of schooling (for example, Apple, 1979; Dreeben, 1968; Henry, 1966; Silberman, 1970; Snyder, 1971). Various writers (for example, Holt, 1964; Hargreaves, 1967; Dreeben, 1968; Jackson, 1968; Illich, 1970) have offered somewhat different versions of the 'hidden curriculum', but all of them have indicated that it interpenetrates with, and is communicated alongside, the official curriculum in teacher–pupil interactions and can be as highly structured and organized, detailed, and complex as the formal curriculum. Henry (1966) points out that communication systems, such as telephones and radios, generate 'noise' along with the official, intended communication. In the classroom the teachers' communications to the pupils – usually communications about the official curriculum – also generate noise. This noise is part of the 'hidden curriculum'. Thus, it has been suggested that this element of the 'hidden curriculum' teaches the pupil norms and values necessary for transition to, and integration into, the adult world (for example, Dreeben, 1968; Haller and Thorsen, 1970), and so an emphasis on socialization – order, control, compliance, and conformity – has been persistently reported (for example, Jackson, 1968; Leacock, 1969; Rist, 1970; Adams and Biddle, 1970). On the other hand, some writers have criticized these implicit qualities as stressing consensus and social orientation not in the best interests of the individual (for example, Henry, 1966; Silberman, 1970; Apple, 1979). Further, the 'hidden curriculum' has been described as a vehicle for possibly unjustified differential treatment of pupils often on the basis of race, academic ability, social class, or gender (for example, Illich, 1970; Rist, 1970; Apple, 1979; Frazier and Sadker, 1973; Hargreaves *et al.*, 1975; Willis, 1977). This interpretation of curriculum – interactions between teachers and pupils, inferred from consistencies in class organization, teacher behaviours, and procedures – has been assumed to have a powerful impact on the values, norms, and behaviour of pupils. In discussing the value system in education Hartley (1985) writes:

> Hitherto, there was little need to formalize the hidden curriculum because its subliminal messages were, for the most part, effectively assimilated. In the main, pupils were adequately socialized by the hidden curriculum to fit into society. Now, however, it appears that pupils cannot be assumed to have acquiesced either in the formal goals of education or in their justification. When teachers justify schooling in vocational terms, the message is questioned by children who know full well that academic credentials are no guarantee of a job ... the meaning of schooling must therefore undergo change.

According to Watkins and Wagner (1987) most teachers view pupils who experience behavioural problems either as culpable authors of their own misfortune or else they are considered to be suffering from a psychologically diagnosed disorder and consider that there is something wrong with the pupil. But Ford, Mangan and Whelan (1982) argue that if we accept this 'pupil deficit' model, attempting to explain away problems in terms of individual pathology, it serves to direct us towards remedial approaches which involve providing alternative provision for the individual or some form of treatment. Yet one of the main conclusions of Rutter *et al.* (1979) is that young people's behaviour and attitudes are shaped and influenced by their experiences at school and, in particular, by the qualities of the school as a social institution. Perhaps this viewpoint can best be understood by referring back to the classic Durkheim (1950) study on criminology in which he asserts that deviant behaviour is not pathological but essentially normal behaviour being designed to respond to particular social circumstances. This is a highly significant point since it shifts the focus from the individual on to the social (and 'hidden') context in which the deviant behaviour takes place. As Watkins and Wagner (1987) argue, disruption is essentially contextual. The maintenance and enhancement of self-esteem is vital to young people and if schools fail to do this, for instance by blocking attainment of valued goals, frustrating status or alienating cultures by employing inappropriate curricula or adopting middle-class bias, then they will be liable to provoke young people into disruptive, hostile or aggressive behaviour (McGuinness, 1989). The author went on to argue that this is precisely what happens to large numbers of pupils in British secondary schools. Those who are successful in areas which are valued by the institution will of course be rewarded and have their self-esteem actually enhanced, and in this connection Claxton (1984) points out that for many pupils, school does work. But for others, school holds out rewards they know they will not get, and do not even want. According to Coleman and Hendry (1990), adolescents may be able to cope with one or two areas of low self-esteem but if there are more areas of failure than of success, then coping will be difficult, creating adverse reaction against the system which can manifest itself in acts of disruption. Raffe (1984) reports the reflections of two 'less academic' school leavers:

> In my eyes they (the teachers) were only interested in the already bright pupils and were not prepared to try to help the unfortunate less bright ones. It was clear that the school wasn't interested in us.

> My teachers made me feel really thick, really stupid so I did not bother to study. They made me feel as if it was not worth my while thinking of what I wanted to be ... so I shall never forget my teachers and how they made me feel.

Schools may be deemed 'comprehensive', though there is a tendency for different schools to view pupils in particular and distinctive ways (Munn *et al.*, 1992). Thus schools can view their pupils predominately as 'scholars' valuing academic achievement and success in public examinations. This would be reflected in classroom organization where the emphasis would be on transmitting subject-specific knowledge, operation of a fairly strict system of hierarchical line management and pastoral care treated as a subject department. Other schools, according to Munn *et al.*, will prioritize the development of pastoral care, undertake more radical programmes of curriculum change and make conscious efforts to view pupils as part of a whole community which includes parents and staff. A third category of school adopts a highly prescriptive regime of rules and sanctions in which pastoral care is effectively reactive 'fire fighting'. These schools would view their pupils as socially deficient. According to Reynolds and Sullivan (1979), schools which try to involve pupils in the life of the school are more successful both in academic terms and in terms of social behaviour. Coercive schools, on the other hand, which are rigid in their discipline, tend to be less successful. Tattum (1982) finds that disruptive children tend to justify their actions within a framework of classroom regulations and procedures by laying blame on teachers who pick on them, treat them with disrespect and apply rules inconsistently. The link between disruption and good teaching, in the sense of sound classroom management, interesting activities, respect for and interest in pupils, is generally accepted (e.g. Elton Committee 1989 in England and Wales, HMI Report 'Effective Secondary Schools' (1988), Scotland).

School to society

The trend through the 1980s and into the 1990s has been to-wards more young people staying on at school beyond the minimum leaving age and going on to further and higher education. National data sets confirm that more middle-class young people stay on to gain better qualifications than work-ing-class adolescents. The association between duration in (secondary) education and post-school careers, however, sug-gests that 'more' does not necessarily mean 'better' in terms of life chances. A combination of structural arrangements within the youth labour market and wider normative con-straints, especially in relation to gender, serve to mitigate the potential effects of additional years in school. Thus for some young people the opportunity to take up an apprenticeship is forfeited in staying on at school an 'extra' year and on leav-ing school such youngsters find themselves in a weaker posi-tion in the labour market as a result. For others staying on at school beyond the minimum school leaving age leads to 'downward status mobility' (in terms of eventual post-school careers) with many moving from 'academic school courses to non-advanced further education ... (or) from school to Youth Training Schemes' (Raffe and Courtenay, 1988) (or) to low status clerical and shop work (Dex, 1987). For women, in particular, additional years at school may pose problems for the reconciling of occupational with domestic career goals.

Educational solutions to the disappearance of jobs for adolescents produce diminishing returns (Bates *et al*, 1984). These attempts to tighten the bonds between schooling and job requirements and to strengthen young people's vocational orientations seem problematic. Holt (1983) argues that the vocational skills of today may well be outdated for use in future society:

> the fact about tomorrow is that it will be different from today, and will present quite new problems. New problems can be solved only by those with the personal and moral autonomy to interpret our culture – by those who have enjoyed a liberal education.

Thus Coleman and Husen (1985) point out that these new educational practices are helping to create a new underclass. They claim that, within secondary schools, a tail-end abandons hope and effort, and sometimes attendance, long before the official leaving date. The majority of young people now leave school with some qualifications, so the 'failures' are a disadvantaged minority.

Concluding remarks

If we are to begin to understand 'disruptive behaviour' in young people; to offer guidelines for effective professional policies for working with young people in schools and other settings in the wider community; and to help young people 'manage' the transitions to adulthood – and their interactions with adults – more effectively, we need to take a wide perspective on the issue of disaffection. This book sets out to do this by illuminating factors and contexts which influence young people's 'positive' and 'disruptive' pathways though school towards adult 'lifeworlds'.

Bibliography

Aaro, L E, Wold, B, Kannas, L and Rimpela, M (1986) Health behaviour in school-children. A WHO cross-national survey. *Health Promotion,* 1, 1, 17–33.

Abel, T and McQueen, D (1992) 'The formation of health lifestyles: a new empirical concept'. Paper presented to the BSA & ESMS Joint Conference on Health in Europe, Edinburgh, 18–21 September 1992.

Adams, R and Biddle, B J (1970) *Realities of Teaching.* New York: Holt, Rinehart, and Winston.

Adams, G R and Gullotta, T (1983) *Adolescent Life Experiences.* California: Brooks-Cole.

Apple, M (1979) 'The hidden curriculum and the nature of conflict', *Interchange* 2: 27–43.

Bates, I, Clarke, J, Cohen, P, Finn, D, Moore, R and Willis, P (1984) *Schooling for the Dole.* London: Macmillan.

Beale, P (1995) Riots blamed on age gap. *The Scotsman,* 12 June, p. 3.

Blyth, D A, Hill, J P and Marlin, M M (1982) Parental and peer influence on adolescents. *Social Forces* 58: 1057–79.

Brake, M (1985) *Comparative Youth Culture.* London: Routledge and Kegan Paul.

Brannen, J, Dodd, K, Oakley, A and Storey, P (1994) *Young People, Health and Family Life.* Buckingham: Open University Press.

Claxton, G (1984) *Live and Learn: An Introduction to the Psychology of Growth and Change in Everyday Life.* London: Harper and Row.

Coffield, F, Borrill, C and Marshall, S (1986) *Growing Up at the Margins.* Milton Keynes: Open University Press.

Coleman, J C (1979) *The School Years* London: Methuen.

Coleman, J C and Hendry, L B (1990) *The Nature of Adolescence.* 2nd Ed. London: Routledge.

Coleman, J S and Husen, T (1985) *Becoming Adult in a Changing Society.* Paris: OECD.

Cooke, R (1995) We're not lost – just growing up. *Sunday Times,* 4 June, 3.6.

Csikszentmihalyi, M (1975) *Beyond Boredom and Anxiety.* San Francisco: Jossey-Bass.

Csikszentmihalyi, M and Larson, R (1984) *Being Adolescent: Conflict and Growth in the Teenage Years.* New York: Basic Books.

Damon, W (1983) *Social and Personality Development: Infancy through Adolescence.* New York: Norton.

Davis, J (1990) *Youth and the Condition of Britain: Images of Adolescent Conflict.* London: Athlone Press.

Devereux, E C (1976) 'Backyard versus little league baseball: the impoverishment of children's play'. In Landers, D (Ed) *Social Problems in Athletics.* Illinois: University of Illinois Press.

Dex, S (1987) *Women's Occupational Mobility.* London: Macmillan.

Docking, J W (1980) *Control and Discipline in Schools.* Harper and Row.

Dreeben, R (1968) *On What is Learned in Schools.* Reading, Mass: Addison-Wesley.

Durkheim, E · (1950) *Suicide: A Study in Sociology.* Routledge, Kegan and Paul.

Elkind, D (1985) Cognitive development and adolescent disabilities. *Journal of Adolescent Health Care,* 6: 84–9.

Elton Report (1989) *Discipline in Schools: Report of the Committee of Enquiry HMSO* (Same as 1988?)

Emler, N (1984) Differential involvement in delinquency: towards an interpretation in terms of reputation management. *Progress in Experimental Personality Research,* 13: 173–239.

Erikson, E (1968) *Identity: youth and crisis.* New York: Norton.

Ford, J, Mangan, D and Whelan, M (1982) *Special Education and Social Control.* Routledge and Kegan Paul.

Frazier, N and Sadker, M (1973) *Sexism in School and Society.* New York: Harper and Row.

Frost, N and Stein, M (1989) *The Politics of Child Welfare.* Brighton: Harvester/Wheatsheaf.

Furlong, V J (1991) Disaffected Pupils: Reconstructing the Sociological Perspective. *British Journal of Sociology of Education.* Volume 12, No. 3.

Giddens, A (1984) *The Constitution of Society.* Oxford: Polity.

Haller, E J and Thorsen, S J (1970) 'The political socialization of children and the structure of the elementary school'. *Interchange* 1: 45–55.

Hargreaves, D H (1967) *Social Relations in a Secondary School.* London: Routledge & Kegan Paul.

Hargreaves, D H, Hester, S K and Mellor, F J (1975) *Deviance in Classrooms.* London: Routledge & Kegan Paul.

Hartley, D (1985) 'Social education in Scotland: some sociological considerations'. *Scottish Educational Review* 17 (2): 92–8.

Hendry, L B (1983) *Growing up and Going out.* Aberdeen: Aberdeen University Press.

Hendry, L B, Glendinning, A, Schucksmith, J, Love, J and Scott, J (1993a) 'The developmental context of adolescent lifestyles'. In Silbereisen, R and Todt, E (Eds). *Adolescents in Context: The Interplay of Family School, Peers and Work in Adjustment.* New York: Springer International.

Hendry, L B, Shucksmith, J, Love, J, Glendinning, A (1993b) *Young People's Leisure and Lifestyles.* London: Routledge.

Hendry, L B (1993) *Learning the New Three Rs?: Educating Young People for Modern Society.* Aberdeen University Review 189, Spring 1993: 33–51.

Hendry, L B and Shucksmith, J (1994) 'Adolescents in the UK'. In Hurrelmann, K (Ed) *International Handbook of Adolescence.* London: Greenwood Press.

Hendry, L B, Shucksmith, J and Philip, K (1995) *Educating for Health.* London: Cassell.

Henry, J (1966) *Culture against Man.* London: Tavistock.

HMSO (1989) *The Children Act.* London: HMSO.

Holt, J (1964) *Why Children Fail.* London: Pitman.

Holt, M (1983) 'Vocationalism: The Next Threat to Universal Education'. *Forum* 25: 84–6.

Hurrelman, K and Losel, F (1990) *Health Hazards in Adolescence.* Berlin and New York: de Gruyter.

Illich, I (1970) *Deschooling Society.* New York: Harper & Row.

Irwin, C E (1989) Risk-taking behaviour in the adolescent patient: are they impulsive? *Paediatric Annals* 18: 122–33.

Irwin, C E and Millstein, S G (1986) Biopsychosocial correlates of risk-taking behaviours during adolescence. *Journal of Adolescent Healthcare* 7: 825–965.

Jack, M S (1989) Personal Fable: A potential explanation for risk-taking behaviour in adolescents. *Journal of Paediatric Nursing* 4: 334–8.

Jackson, P W (1968) *Life in Classrooms.* New York: Holt, Rinehart and Winston.

Jessor, R (1991) Risk behaviour in adolescence: a psychosocial framework for understanding and action. Personal communication quoted in Plant, M and Plant, M (1992) *Risk Takers, Alcohol, Drugs, Sex and Youth.* London: Routledge.

Kaplan, H B (1980) *Deviant Behaviour in Defense of Self.* New York: Academic Press.

Kreppner, K and Lerner, R M (1989) Family systems and lifespan development. In Kreppner, K and Lerner, R M (Eds). *Issues and Perspectives in Family Systems and Lifespan Development.* Hillsdale, New Jersey: Erlbaum.

Lawrence, J, Steed, D, Young, P and Hilton, G (1981) *Dialogue on Disruptive Behaviour: A Study of a Secondary School.* London: PJP Press.

Leacock, E B (1969) *Teaching and Learning in City Schools.* New York: Basic Books.

Lloyd, M A (1985) *Adolescence.* London: Harper & Row.

Marsland, D (1987) *Education and Youth.* London: Falmer Press.

Montemayor, R and van Komen, R (1986) Age segregation of adolescents in and out of school. *Journal of Youth and Adolescents* 9: 371–81.

Munn, P, Johnstone, M and Chalmers, V (1992) *Effective Discipline in Secondary Schools and Classrooms.* Paul Chapman.

Murdock, G and Phelps, F (1973) *Mass Media and the Secondary School.* London: Macmillan.

Neil, A (1995) The poor may be richer but the underclass is growing. *Sunday Times* 28 May, 3, 5.

Oldman, D (1994) Adult–child relations as class relations. In Qvortrup, J, Bardy, M, Sgritta, G and Wintersberger, H (Eds) *Childhood Matters.* Aldershot: Avebury.

Qvortrup, J (1994) Childhood matters: An introduction. In Qvortrup, J, Bardy, M, Sgritta, G and Wintersberger, H (Eds) *Childhood Matters.* Aldershot: Avebury.

Petersen, A C, Ebatta, A T and Graber, J A (1987) 'Coping with adolescence: the functions and disfunctions of poor achievement'. Paper presented at the biennial meeting of the Society of Research in Child Development, Baltimore, Maryland.

Plant, M and Plant, M (1992) *Risk-takers, Alcohol, Drugs, Sex and Youth.* London: Routledge.

Raffe, D (1984) *Fourteen to Eighteen.* Aberdeen University Press.

Raffe, D and Courtenay, G (1988) '16–18 on both sides of the border'. In Raffe, D (Ed) *Education and the Youth Labour Market.* London: Falmer Press

Reynolds, D and Sullivan, M (1979) Bringing schools back in. In Barton, L and Meighan, R (Eds) *Schools, Pupils and Deviance.* Driffield: Nafferton Books.

Rist, R G (1970) 'Student social class and teacher expectations: the self-fulfilling prophesy in ghetto education. *Harvard Educational Review* 40: 411–51.

Roberts, K (1984) *School Leavers and Their Prospects.* Milton Keynes: Open University Press.

Roberts, K and Parsell, G (1990). 'Young people's routes into UK labour markets in the late 1980s'. Occasional paper 27, ESRC 16–19 initiative. London: City University.

Rutter, M *et al.* (1979) *Fifteen Thousand Hours: Secondary Schools and their Effects on Children.* Open Books.

Rutter, M and Smith, D (1995) *Psychosocial Disorders in Young People: Time Trends and Their Causes.* London: Wiley.

Seccombe, W (1993) *Weathering the Storm.* London: Verso.

Silbereisen, R K, Noack, P and Eyferth, K (1987) 'Place for development: adolescents leisure settings and developmental tasks'. *In* Silbereisen, R K, Eyferth, K and Rudinger, G (Eds). *Development as Action in Context: Problem Behaviour and Normal Youth Development.* New York: Springer.

Silberman, C E (1970) *Crisis in the Classroom.* New York: Vintage Books.

Simmons, R, Rosenberg, F and Rosenberg, M (1973) 'Disturbance in the self-image of adolescents'. *American Sociological Review* 38: 553–68.

Snyder, B R (1971) *The Hidden Curriculum.* New York: Knopf.

Tattum, D P (1982) *Disruptive Pupils in Schools and Units.* Wiley and Sons.

Topping, K J (1983) *Education Systems for Disruptive Adolescents.* London: Croom Helm.

Wadsworth, M (1979) *Roots of Delinquency.* Oxford: Martin Robertson and Co. Ltd.

Wallace, C (1986) 'From girls and boys to women and men: the social reproduction of gender roles in the transition from school to (un)employment'. In Walker, S and Barton, L (Eds). *Youth Unemployment and Schooling.* Milton Keynes: Open University Press.

Watkins, C and Wagner, P (1987) *School Discipline: A Whole School Approach.* Blackwell.

Wenzel, R (1982) 'Health promotion and lifestyles: perspectives of the WHO Regional Office for Europe, Health

Education Programme'. Paper presented to the 11th International Conference on Health Education, Tasmania.

Wheldall, K and Merrett, F (1984) *Positive Teaching: The Behavioural Approach.* London: Allen and Unwin.

Willis, P E (1977) *Learning to Labour.* Farnborough: Saxon House.

Zieman, G L and Benson, G P (1983) 'Delinquency: the role of self esteem and self values'. *Journal of Youth and Adolescence,* 12 (6): 489–99.

2 Victims of exclusion: their voice

Callum

I went to a small nursery and infant primary school. I was very happy there. The teachers looked after me and I had lots of friends.

My dad left us just after my seventh birthday. I hated him and was glad to see him go. There were always fights and rows when he was around.

It was about the time dad left us that I went to the junior school. It seemed so big – and so did the boys at the top end of the school. They picked on me every break time but I've always been able to take care of myself. Had to with a dad like mine. But the ******** kept reporting me to the head. They started the fights but the head always blamed me. The teachers were alright but I reckon the head had it in for me as soon as he set eyes on me. I can see it all now. Them boys got me so mad I just kept lashing out at them. The headteacher always took their side, never mine. It seemed like every break and every lunchtime I got into scrapes and then the old ******* would punish me. It were really odd. I got on OK during lessons but I couldn't keep it together outside.

When I started at the secondary school I decided to keep it together. The first two years they didn't bother me too much. But then it went wrong. It wasn't my fault. They kept getting me at breaks and you just have to fight back. I had to see the headteacher every week – sometimes every day. It wasn't my fault, it never was but they'd never listen. You know what he did? Yeah, of course the bloody headteacher. He kicked me out. Expelled. My ma went crazy but it was no good the ******* wouldn't have me back. He wouldn't even listen. It's nae fair, they wouldn't listen. They just pushed me out. I never did get back into a secondary school.

I went to a funny little place at first but the staff are great. They're strict but they talk to you normal like – and they listen. I've liked being here and I haven't got into any real trouble but if I had another go in school I'd want them (the teachers) to treat me straight. P'raps I shouldn't have pushed 'em so hard.

I have lots of things I do outside of school – mainly sport. I have lots of friends. All my mates are lads. I used to go around with some girls but they can't get enough of me and won't leave me alone so I've just had to give them up.

John

What did they (parents) ever do for me – I hate them. Me dad left us when I was a baby – I hate him for it. I'll kill him one day. The old lady's not much better. She never wanted me. We're allus fighting and she doesn't care what I do, where I go to or anything just so long as I'm not at home. As soon as I get a job I'm leaving.

I've hated all my time at school. I did go to a nursery school but I don't remember anything about it, maybe it was better. Primary school was terrible – teachers and classmates had got it in for me. I didn't like what we had to do, the lessons were always boring. I didn't do much work but the teachers would get angry with me for no reason and then I'd give them a bit o' lip. Classmates used to laugh when I sounded off at the teacher and she'd get real angry. It helped with the fights at break. After I played up the teacher I didn't get roughed up in the playground so much. But nobody liked me – everybody picked on me.

Things didn't change much at secondary school. I was in trouble on day one. The teachers picked on me but I thumped one of them and then I was expelled. I don't blame 'em really. I shouldn't have thumped him. They sent me to another secondary school. The discipline was much tougher but I used to get picked on 'til I started leading this gang. We went after another school's gang one lunchtime. There were 30 or 40 of us and this massive gang came out to meet us. But we showed 'em. When I went back into class I had blood dripping from me 'ead but me mates were cheering. It weren't long after this I got kicked out. I never went back to a proper school.

I know I should be better if I had my time in school again but I get a real buzz out there being the leader. Like leading the gang or breaking into houses. It's good while it's happening and it's good when you get caught. Most of the people round here think I'm stupid but they're the ones who's stupid. They're rough and dirty and they just don't know what's going on. Me and me mates we know what to do. We like telly, playing pool and going to Rollerland to pick up girls. I've got lots of mates but I'm not telling *you* who they are.

Linda

I get on with my parents OK but mum bawls a lot. She frightens me when she's like that and I have to get out of her way. I'm a bit like that at school. If anyone shouts like that I try to get away.

I went to school very young and it was good. I used to like the Wendy house best. I had lots of friends at primary school but I was always given baby work to do and I spent less and less time with them. When I went to secondary school I didn't see much of them at all but I went round with another girl. We got on really great together and I don't know how it started but we got into trouble with the teachers. After that we couldn't do anything right. Teachers picked on us. I did swear at some teachers but only when they asked for it and yeah I did hit two teachers but they started it. They excluded me. We had meetings at school and my parents couldn't see that I'd been picked on – they took sides with the teachers. Anyway I went to another set-up. There aren't many pupils but the teachers are good. They listen to you and are good fun to be with.

Elizabeth

I don't know why you keeping asking me about my dad, he never did anything for us. Mum's bad enough. She's always shouting, telling me off and in a lousy mood. The slightest thing and I get sent to bed and sometimes I'm grounded for up to two weeks. But he never did anything.

Lately, since mum remarried, things have got easier. She's in a better mood and he (stepfather) doesn't bother me much.

I don't know whether I went to a nursery school but primary school was great. I had lots of friends and the teachers were really easy to speak to. When mum remarried we moved house and I had to move schools. The teachers there weren't very nice and not very easy to speak to. At first nobody liked me but I soon got lots of mates and we took on the other gang. None of their lot could frighten me. But I never got into real trouble at primary school.

Secondary school seemed so big to start with. I enjoyed most of the subjects and I think some of the teachers cared about me. But none of them were easy to speak to. I got by in the first year but then it all went wrong. Teachers started picking on me – why was I late? Why hadn't I handed my homework in. Why hadn't I got this or that done during their precious lesson? All the time. It was nae my fault that they expected too much work. But then they did it. Kept setting me lines and books to write out. I got so angry. The other pupils didn't make it any better neither. They'd skit me about the way I looked and always being in trouble in class. I had to hit back. If I got skitted I used to hit them. Once it got so bad that while we were scrapping some chairs and tables got smashed. Do-yer-know I was the only one that got excluded. They had me back but I was out for over two weeks that time. I couldn't help it when I got back to school – anyone who got in my way or tried I'd 'it 'em. They kicked me out for good and I went to this place in the city. There weren't many pupils but the teachers were really easy to speak to.

If I had my time at school again I'd want teachers who are really easy to speak to and who weren't picking on you.

I have lots of friends. Friends are people who muck around with you and stick by you. I've got one close friend but we had a fight and we're not speaking at the moment.

Neil

I know I'm big but that's no reason for the others picking on me all the time. It started when I started school. Someone pinched my crisps so I hit him. It wasn't my fault – he shouldn't have stolen my crisps. Everything seemed to follow on from that, lots of incidents, but I always got the blame. I hadn't sent that note round about the headteacher. The whole of my time in primary school was like that – I always got the blame. It was the primary headteacher, he always had it in for me – that's why I didn't get to a proper secondary school.

I had to go to this residential school but it's been good for me. I've got some good mates. We like drinking and driving cars. I'm going to look for a job which has something to do with cars or bikes when I get out of here.

Wilma

When I was little we all lived together and there didn't seem to be any sort of problem. I was happy at home and I can't remember any unhappiness at the infant or junior schools I went to. I had friends in my classes and I liked me teachers.

I don't know when it started but I remember thinking one day that it had been a long time since my parents had a day without a row. I blamed her. She could be so nasty. She'd swear at him and call him names. He couldn't cope with it. She could be quite violent too. When he left she turned on me. It was all my fault you see so she used to beat me and she'd swear at me. That's when the social worker came. She took me to a home. I didn't like it much but I wasn't there long before I went to my gran's. Things seemed to slowly get better then. I can see it now. I was all mixed up but moving to the residential school and weekends at gran's was good for me.

I came to the residential school from secondary school – my second secondary school. The first one had been alright. I'd moved with my friends and I was happy. Then my parents started having rows and fights and it was sometime then when I had to go to the home. I hated my mother. I kicked and screamed at the social worker – she took me to another school. I didn't find any friends. I was lonely and miserable and it was all their fault. The other pupils called me names and I began to get into fights with the other girls. I hurt someone badly and so I was sent here (residential EBD school).

I hated this school to start with. I wanted to go home and they wouldn't let me. I gave them a hard time but they didn't expel me. I feel now that it was right for me at the time but I wish I hadn't come here.

My main interest is football. I watch the Dons but I go on my own. My cousin is my best friend because she's the only friend who is not two-faced.

Ian

Of all the pupils interviewed Ian found the process the most difficult. He did not make eye contact once and did not sit down for more than 30 seconds at any one time. Ian said little more than yes or no to the various questions and the picture which emerged was one he wished to believe and had little relation to reality.

Life at home is great. I get on with both my mum and dad. Father is boss and mum looks after us all very well. She is always patient and kind.

I know I was lazy at school but I couldn't help it. I was lazy at primary school and nobody pushed me. The teachers would talk to you and help you but none of them tried to get me to do more work. When I moved to secondary school the speed of working was much faster so I just got further and further behind. The teachers weren't very helpful – they kept picking on me and trying to get me to do the work. It used to worry me at first but I soon started answering them back. I'm lazy and that's that. What I needed was a school that wasn't going to push you into anything that you didn't want to do. This residential school is like that but I would rather be at home.

My family are great. I have three close friends and we like going to the football at the weekend.

Sandy

Ever since I can remember dad worked off-shore so I used to see him every two weeks. By the time dad was due to come home mum would be off the wall. Anyway when she couldn't cope with it any longer they split up. It meant moving schools and I hated that. But mum is easy to get round. She'll let me do anything I want. So I just didn't go to school and that's when I started getting into trouble. I didn't really understand what were happening but it seemed ages since I had seen my mum and dad and then the social worker came round. I was sent to a children's home and then to Oakbank (*residential school*).

I was frightened to start with. I didn't know why I was here or how long I was going to be kept here. That was two years ago. The staff here are really good. They seem more disappointed than angry when you get into trouble. But I still can't help it – if my mates take off I have to go with them. I don't like it when the police pick us up and somehow it's even worse when I get back here and have to tell the staff why I did a runner. I know I'm going to lose time at home when I run but I can't stop going with my mates.

I have lots of interests but they're mainly to do with sport. I like playing but I can't sit still long enough to watch much telly. Jimmy my best mate tells me that when I watch telly I keep moving from chair to chair.

I don't know what I'm going to do when I leave here next week. Maybe my mum will take me back in.

Ricky

I don't like doing this sort of thing because you're never sure what the right answer is. What happens if I get it wrong – never mind I'll have a go anyway.

I like being here (*residential school*) better than home. My real dad left us years ago and I don't get on with my new dad. Mum's alright when she gives me money but most of the time she just shouts at me. She used to have ****** silly rules about what time I had to be in and who I could go out with. She'd get real mad if I wasn't in on time. It's the same here – they have rules but they don't yell and scream if you're caught out – you lose home leave and get put on report.

Primary school was OK. I had loads of friends and the work was easy. I went to two schools an' I got on fine at both of 'em. The teachers were nice and used to look after you properly. They never set too much homework. Secondary teachers were always shouting and most of them were big-headed. They set loads of homework. I could never keep up.

It's good here. The teachers do lots of sport and I've got lots of friends. I enjoy sport and I wouldn't mind doing something with sport when I leave school.

David

I don't know my father. He took off when I was born. Good riddance. Mum and I get by. Mum lets me come and go as I please so we get on fine.

Oakbank's (*residential school*) alright but I hated primary and secondary schools. The teachers called me names in front of the class and after I had seen them doctors (*psychologist and psychiatrist*) everyone used to call me names. They can't do that here because they've all got one.

The stories of ten permanently excluded pupils

The ten pupils, whose stories were extrapolated from the work of Sanders (1990), had been permanently excluded from mainstream schools, and were in the final two weeks of statutory schooling. The pupils, seven boys and three girls, were chosen from volunteers from four different types of alternative provision. These included two residential schools and two types of part-time provision: one operating as an off-site school unit and the second mainly biased towards individual tuition programmes. All had a main aim of re-integrating pupils into mainstream but in the case of the pupils interviewed this had not proved possible.

The main purpose of interviewing the ten pupils was to obtain some insight into their perception of mainstream education, exclusion and placement in alternative education. The interview also provided an opportunity to examine their responses through the pupil questionnaire which they had completed along with over 3000 other pupils from both primary and secondary mainstream schools (discussion of the returns of mainstream pupils follows in the next chapter). It also enabled more detailed discussion about their leisure interests, aspirations for the future and their friends.

Generally the pupils' family situations seem to have been difficult and on occasions traumatic. Of the ten pupils, only two described their family situations as happy and it could be argued one of these was not receiving adequate support from her family. It was also observed that times of significant and adverse changes in the family situation coincided with periods of the most intense difficulty the pupil experienced at school. This is not to suggest that conflict in the home will always lead to pupils being disruptive, but for these ten pupils, defined as being disruptive, the majority have experienced considerable difficulties in the home situation. This is well represented by some of the pupils own comments. Wilma blamed her mother for all 'the many hurts' she had experienced, while John, who had been completely rejected by his father commented with great vehemence 'I'll kill him one day'.

In terms of early education few of the pupils had recollections of pre-school provision and those who did, appeared to have fond memories of that particular period of their life. Reactions to primary school varied considerably. Half the group had generally enjoyed their primary school experience and the other half had reacted against it, which was made manifest by behaviour at school or simply truanting. The most acrimonious recollections of primary school life were summed up by David who when commenting on his best time at primary school replied 'the day I left'. Although David's response was the most extreme, it would appear from the pupils' account of their primary education, and the supporting evidence, that at least seven of the pupils' potential degree of difficulty could have been identified at the primary stage. It also appeared from their case histories that the intensity of the problem had to peak at a high level before a review of their case took place and a different type of education was provided. Primary schools had attempted to cope with these pupils' disruptive behaviour but, given the outcome, generally without any significant degree of success. Perhaps the introduction of the Code of Practice (DFE 1994) and the development of an Individual Education Plan (see Chapter 5) would provide a better chance of maintaining a mainstream place or at least provide a more appropriate pathway to alternative educational opportunities.

Clearly the delivery of education at primary school is substantially different from that at a secondary school. Class teachers will figure very highly in the life of a primary-aged pupil and therefore the individual class teacher will have a significant role in pupils' acceptance of primary education. Four of the ten pupils had poor recollections of their primary class teachers and their most common comments reflected a perception of teachers lacking empathy with their pupils. Elizabeth, for example, kept repeating the phrase that she liked teachers who were 'really easy to speak to'. Neil repeated the view shared by most of his peers of having been 'picked on' by many of his teachers.

Translating these pupil perceptions to the secondary situation, all pupils had some adverse comments to make about their secondary schooling – particularly about being picked on. Other comments referred to the pressures of academic work, the size of the school, and the difficulty they had relating to the teachers. Two of the ten pupils interviewed had not transferred into a mainstream secondary school at any stage but for the remaining eight considerable difficulty was experienced in the transition from primary to secondary. For these eight pupils the ultimate sanction of permanent exclusion occurred in their respective secondary schools and this is likely to have coloured their recollection of the mainstream secondary school. However, all of the pupils had some difficulty in believing that their actions and misbehaviour justified them being excluded. Most echoed Graham's view of 'was nae fair' and of having been picked on. Being picked on did not refer just to the teachers but also to their peers who 'goaded' them into fights. Physical and verbal abuse was a common theme, many agreeing with the comment made by Elizabeth in which she suggested that eventually a point was reached when 'she could only go on fighting back'. This propensity towards a physical reaction was a recurring theme in the pupils' background reports. Also evident from the reports was schools' treatment of pupils involved in physical incidents. This always led to the application of sanctions but a disinclination to seek alternative means of managing their behaviour – again perhaps the Code of Practice will in the future provoke a different response.

At the time of the interviews the ten pupils were placed in four different types of alternative provision. Nine of the ten pupils considered the educational provision was appropriate and to their liking. They felt the teachers in such establishments had both empathy and time for them as pupils. They were easy to talk to and were often genuinely disappointed when the pupils did not respond positively. The ten pupils' main criticism of their provision was in relation to those who were placed in a residential school. This was seen as an unnecessarily tough punishment compared with their perception of the reasons for the permanent exclusion – even if they had been the prime instigator of the disruption for which largely they did not accept any responsibility. Other pupils did express some concern about the limitations of the curriculum and certification.

All of the pupils felt that it was important to have a large circle of friends but many of them found it difficult to describe what they meant by a friend. Some indicated that they had a large circle of friends but were unable (or unwilling) to give names of such friends or the amount of time which they spent with them. Eight of the ten pupils were aggressive in their peer relationships and few of the pupils had extensive leisure interests – mainly 'hanging around', and it was thought that these two factors may account for the apparent small circle of friends of each excluded pupil. Relationships with the opposite sex figured quite strongly in responses but the degree of stability and success of such relationships was somewhat over-exaggerated. Callum, for example, when talking about his friendships with girls replied, 'Girls can't get enough of me and won't leave me alone so I've just had to give them up.'

All ten pupils were, at the time of the interview, within two weeks of their school leaving date. They were asked to reflect upon the time they had spent in schools and the events leading to their exclusion. All seemed to regret having been removed from mainstream education and most felt aggrieved about their permanent exclusion. Four of the ten considered that it was the fault of their peers, teachers or the headteacher that they had been excluded and that it had nothing to do with their own behaviour. Several of the others commented that if they were able to have their time at school again they would hope to behave differently but felt it was unlikely they would have been successful. Ian, for example, when considering this question thought that history would repeat itself because 'I'm just lazy and that's that.'

Summary of the victims' cases

In reviewing the case histories of these ten excluded pupils a common picture emerged. The pupils were all of below average ability and most had difficult home circumstances. The lack of the pupils' ability to form relationships, knowledge of social requirements and low academic performance was often recognizable in the primary phase, but it would appear that behaviour had to deteriorate markedly before any additional support was requested or an alternative strategy attempted. Relocation of pupils to alternative provision had been a curative response to crisis situations. Such crises leading to exclusion occurred most commonly in the secondary schools. Given the amount of work that the ten excluded pupils created for teachers and senior staff in mainstream schools, it is perhaps ironic that the most preferred qualities of teachers by the ten pupils were empathy and good class control.

How does this compare with the reaction of pupils in mainstream schools? Do the less able pupils have a predilection to disruption? What do pupils think are the most important characteristics of a good teacher? Does the character of each individual pupil have any bearing on his or her ability to keep out of trouble? In Chapter 3 we consider the responses of over 3000 primary and secondary pupils to these and other issues.

3   Causal factors of disruption: the missing ingredient?

If you are academic you get homework. If you are in 4x you do not. Pupils are not daft. They have feelings too. Why do able pupils need homework when the less able do not? Surely educationists could make a cogent argument for it being the other way round.

(Reid, 1987)

Introduction

Does the regime in schools help *all* pupils to succeed or does the day to day practice exaggerate the differences between the most able and better behaved pupils and their less privileged counterparts? Reid (1986, 1987) expressed his concern that schools were not meeting the needs of pupils with a record of low achievement and poor self-esteem. Such pupils commonly vote with their feet and by so doing exacerbate their own problems of low academic performance and a low self-perception. We all need to feel good about ourselves, to have a positive attitude and to have a modicum of success, otherwise we begin to feel undervalued or even failures in terms of the demands which society makes upon us. This can affect the ego or self-image adversely and reduce self-confidence and self-esteem. If failure becomes more of the norm, then it is hardly surprising that adolescents become disaffected and challenge authority whether that be parents, the community, the school or society at large (Lawrence *et al.*, 1984; Reid, 1987; Sanders, 1990; Ruddock *et al.*, 1996).

In the case of pupils such disillusion, and likely underachievement, has the potential of becoming a vicious circle. If adolescents lack confidence and self-esteem they are more prone to underachieve or fail. If their level of achievement is low or relatively low, aspirations on their behalf may be lowered. In turn this may become part of a self-fulfilling prophecy (Jones, 1977; Reid, 1987; Sanders, 1990).

The literature examined in Chapter 1 demonstrates the range of factors which may influence the response and attitude of young people. These include the home and family circumstances, the regime of the school, peer pressure, the local community and cultural setting, and societal parameters, particularly levels of employment. Within each of these areas a range of parameters will come into play. The school setting, for example, will vary with the personalities of the teaching staff; the quality of the management team; the expectations placed on pupils; the nature of peer pressure, etc. Young people are exposed to a multifaceted and dynamic situation in which a number of these influences can separately or collectively interact and impact on their behaviour – either positively or negatively. Research has concentrated on attempting to prove causal links between the attributes of young people (e.g. academic performance, behaviour) and the major areas of potential influence (e.g. school, home, peer pressure). These have provided statistically meaningful data for analysis in an attempt to prove the key influences which cause young people to become disaffected and disruptive. However, within this process there is a tendency to lose the views of the individual and nullify their importance. The authors do not suggest that analysis of 'whole' systems to establish causal factors of disaffection is inappropriate or wrong, but would wish to highlight the danger of camouflaging the perspective of the individual and thereby losing the essential element of the issue of disruption – the pupil.

Past research has reflected a predilection for identifying a causal link between disruption and home and family circumstances on the one hand and school on the other. However, with school, not all children from lower socio-economic families have low academic achievements and not all children from slum areas become delinquents. Indeed this is far from being the case. So, if the children from very similar backgrounds react differently to the same situations, there must be a further parameter of importance. Young people have thoughts, feelings, attitudes, attributes and personalities of their own. Like adults, for some their character will help them to keep out of any real difficulty and for others it will be the reverse. This chapter looks at young people and their views and examines how their feelings about themselves influences behaviour. Inherent within this approach is the danger that one perceived causal factor, such as home or school, is being replaced with another – pupil self-esteem. The authors recognize this risk but would suggest that for every disruptive pupil each of these three causal factors is present to a greater or lesser extent and interact dynamically according to the character and attributes of the individual.

Graham

Graham is the youngest child of a family of five. The family lived in a poor dock-side area (locally known as 'over the marsh') in a small three-bedroomed terraced house more remarkable for its smell than the architectural design. Graham's brothers and sisters all attended the local primary school and while they did not distinguish themselves, they managed to pass through the school without blemish and transfer to the local secondary school. However, Graham's extremely poor ability in reading and writing led to some doubts about his transfer to secondary school. His situation was reviewed by the parents, teachers and educational psychologist who jointly agreed that Graham should remain in primary school for an additional year.

While such a decision is much less likely today because of earlier intervention through the Code of Practice (DFE, 1994), its impact on Graham is still worthy of consideration. Prior to the implementation of this decision, Graham though extremely poor academically was well behaved both with teachers and peers. However, following being 'kept down a year' his behaviour deteriorated rapidly and his academic performance plummeted. He failed to maintain even his very low standards in language and number work. He became physically aggressive to his new peers and started swearing at, and being unco-operative with, his teachers. Characteristics which had not been part of Graham's previous behavioural pattern. His class teacher employed a number of strategies to help Graham but none were successful. Graham's behaviour had deteriorated so badly that consideration was being given to his permanent exclusion and possible admission into a 'special' school. Just as Graham's situation was sinking to its lowest ebb, the school launched a new after-school activity – archery. While Graham's membership of the new club caused many an anxious moment for the teacher in charge Graham responded positively to the sport and started to succeed. For years he had been weak not only intellectually but also in every other area of social and sporting life within the school. He became very involved with the sport, eventually becoming the school champion and the club's captain. His confidence soared and his personality blossomed. The change in Graham's self-esteem was evident and with it his ability to cope academically and socially. Graham's propensity for disruption diminished and his school work improved.

Self-esteem and disaffection: an inverse relationship?

While Graham's family and social circumstances had severe limitations these, in his case, did not appear to have causal links with his disaffection and consequent disruptive behaviour. The professionals involved agreed that the evident deterioration in Graham's behaviour was a direct consequence of being kept down in primary school and as a result, his plummeting self-esteem. The improvement in Graham's behaviour was as marked as its sudden deterioration and both appeared to be inversely related to his self-esteem at that time. While it may be argued that Graham's deteriorating behaviour was a product of the headteacher's intervention and therefore a school-related factor, such an approach misses the subtleties and importance of Graham's self-esteem in his subsequent behaviour. Without structural changes, changes of staff or rules in the school Graham's attitude and behaviour improved beyond recognition. Perhaps it was just one of those things. Perhaps it was something much more fundamental and a pupil's self-image is a key factor in determining a pupil's predilection for disruption.

The significance of self-esteem in the development of children and adolescents has been highlighted extensively in the literature through the last two decades (Epstein, 1973; Rosenberg, 1979; Harter, 1983; Coleman and Hendry, 1990). The main influential characteristics include:

1. Competence, or success in meeting achievement demands.
2. Social acceptance or acceptance, worthiness, and positive reinforcement received from others.
3. Control, or feelings of internal responsibility for outcome.
4. Virtue, or adherence to moral and ethical standards.

(Coleman and Hendry, 1990)

Young people who perceive themselves as high achievers in these four areas are likely to have a good self-image and positive self-esteem. It is argued that success enhances self-esteem and increases self-confidence. Success can provide the momentum through which new challenges can be accepted with alacrity and turned into new successes, although failure can also have a positive outcome if it generates a determination to be more successful in the future:

where failure becomes the norm it may destroy self-esteem. Poor self-esteem and waning self-confidence are prerequisites of disenchantment and provide a route to disaffection. Is it surprising that pupils who perceive themselves as failures become disillusioned, disaffected and perhaps disruptive? Schools provide a competitive environment in which pupil performance is measured and commented upon. Some of the messages are overt and some covert but all have a potential impact on pupil self-image.

The literature on *pupils'* self-image and self-concept and its importance in behavioural responses may appear to create a picture which is in conflict with disruptive behaviour being closely associated with the home or the school. Research has been much devoted to the examination of such causal links, but by comparison very little has been done to statistically represent the views of the individual. This book attempts to draw these polarizations together and includes highlights of the perceptions of over 3000 young people.

The Scottish study (see Appendix A) included responses to a questionnaire (Appendix B) from 1776 primary school pupils and 1303 secondary pupils. Additionally, the ten excluded pupils (see Chapter 2) completed questionnaires as a part of their interviews. While it is recognized that the sample of ten pupils is too small to be of statistical significance their responses have been included for comparative purposes. The main emphases of the questionnaire related to the pupils' perception of family, school and themselves. The responses of mainstream pupils were correlated with the teachers' view of each pupil's propensity for disruption. Additionally pupils' views were sought on the attributes of good teachers and the worst punishments which could be given by their teachers.

Pupils' view – family relationships

The first part of the questionnaire (see Appendix B) asked pupils about their family life. Their responses showed that almost all of the pupils surveyed lived with their natural mother (98 per cent primary, 97 per cent secondary, 90 per cent special),but a significant minority did not live with their natural father (20 per cent primary, 20 per cent secondary, 70 per cent special).

The distribution of father's occupation by percentage of 'known' returns is shown below.

	Pupils from		
	Primary	Secondary	Special
Social class 1	7	5	
2	20	21	20
3	39	44	20
4	21	22	10
5	8	4	10
Unemployed	5	4	40

Both primary and secondary pupils had very positive responses to questions on family relationships – 91 per cent felt that they related well to both mother and father, and over 97 per cent said they related well to their mother. A small minority (<10 per cent) of the pupils felt that parents were too strict and most (>90 per cent) were allowed to bring friends home and parents wished to know where they were going to out of school. Pupils were fairly evenly divided about the extent of parental responsibilities, with 54 per cent believing that once they were away from home what they 'got up to' was their business and not their parents'. The responses of the two groups, primary and secondary, were remarkably similar.

Regarding the ten pupils who had been excluded, the majority (60 per cent) felt that they had good relationships with their parents. A minority (40 per cent) of pupils considered mothers to be too strict. Responses regarding the impact of fathers were limited because only three of the pupils had their natural fathers at home. Most (80 per cent) pupils were allowed to bring friends home and similarly 80 per cent of pupils indicated that parents wished to know where they were going to at night. Only one of the pupils indicated categorically that parents should have jurisdiction over their children's out of school activities. Of the ten pupils only four believed their parents to be proud of them and only one thought they received any support from parents with homework – compared with 74 per cent of primary and 70 per cent of secondary pupils.

The contrast between the 'norms' of mainstream pupils and the ten excluded pupils is evident. The likelihood of both natural parents being together and providing a home for the excluded pupil was much lower. Similarly it was much more likely that the pupils' parents would be unemployed or of lower socio-economic status. As stated earlier the sample of 'special' pupils was very small and therefore it would not be appropriate to generalize from such a limited sample. However, the pupils' parental occupations were correlated against teachers' perception of their propensity for disruption. The results of the survey of mainstream pupils are summarized in Figure 3.1. The patterns of return reflect a variable picture for both primary and secondary female pupils but for boys, and particularly for secondary school boys, there appears to be a clearly increasing pattern of pupil propensity for disruption against reduced occupational status of parents.

Does this mean that home circumstances are strongly associated with a pupil's propensity for disruption or exclusion? The numbers are small and therefore it is inappropriate to generalize but these results reflect some of the outcomes of Coleman's (1966) work which suggests a close relationship between children's behaviour and performance, and their home circumstances. Research on the significance of the child's home background in establishing behavioural and per-formance patterns, particularly in their formative years, places great emphasis on the need for a caring, stable and consistent environment and it is suggested that these are paramount in a child's upbringing. Studies of children who have not had this type of upbringing suggest that the children are not so responsive to adult intervention,

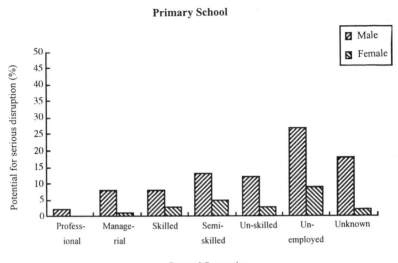

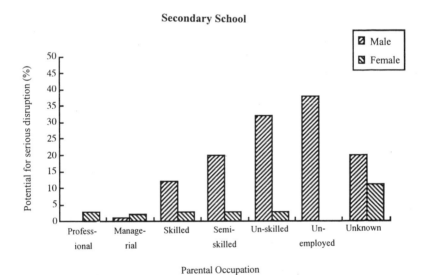

Figure 3.1: Relationship between pupil potential for serious disruption and parental occupation.

have a tendency towards physical and verbal abuse and are generally much more difficult to control and to 'socialize'. Do these results from the Scottish study reinforce the perspective of home being the causal link with pupil propensity for disruption?

Research (Docking, 1980; Watt and Flett, 1985) does reflect children's need of a stable environment in order to thrive – but not necessarily the family home, providing that not being at home is not perceived as rejection. Where both parents are going to work it has been shown to be important that the parents, and the mother in particular, need to have some degree of job satisfaction so that employment is seen by all as positive (Docking, 1980).

Tizard and Hughes (1984) and Watt and Flett (1985) suggested a role for the parents, and mothers in particular, as the 'Prime Educators'. The theme, similar to that of Heath and Clifford (1980), is that children will spend the majority of their time in the family setting and be affected by the role that adults adopt – particularly the parents and particularly the mothers in the child's pre-school years. Understandably, the quality of the input by parents will relate in part to their own self-perception.

> The key factor ... seems to be the power and prestige which mothers feel in their role.
>
> (Watt and Flett, 1985)

Where the mother has high self-perception and feels valued in her role, the better the environment she will create for her child. The needs of the child will be assessed more accurately and provision and stimulation will be provided more appropriately to meet these needs (McCail, 1981). The perceptions of the mother will relate to her own circumstances and how she is regarded in the family (Watt and Flett, 1985). Earlier research (Roberts in Craft *et al.*, 1980) suggests that this will relate quite closely to the social status of the family.

... middle class parents do not treat success as a prize reserved for the intellectually brilliant but act on the assumption that it lies within the grasp of any industrious child of their own ...

... working class parents ... accept signs of failure that a child lacks the required ability.

(Roberts, 1980)

The argument that the home and family circumstances have significant impact on the child's behaviour and performance seem quite powerful and appear to be supported by the findings of the Scottish study.

That home and family influence behavioural responses of children, particularly young children, is not being questioned. However, the subtleties of how this occurs and whether this influence is the key causal factor is under debate. The crux of the argument being put forward is that in a positive situation children can feel good about themselves – can have high self-esteem and self-concept, through which self-confidence will develop. The factors which will influence an individual in this respect will include home and family circumstances but will also include a myriad of other parameters such as peer responses which will increase in importance as the child enters adolescence and outside influences impinge on the child, including the school. However, each of these factors impacts on the individual who consciously or inadvertently will act and react to their influence. The nature of each individual's abilities, attributes and personality traits does vary enormously as will the way in which they respond to all of these 'external forces'.

The ten excluded pupils clearly had home circumstances which were not as good, but perhaps more importantly were perceived by the ten pupils as not being as good, as many of their peers. If this is the key causal factor in their poor behavioural record leading to exclusion from school then a lot of pupils, not least of whom would be their own brothers and sisters, should by definition also ultimately have been excluded from school. While the number of pupils who have been permanently excluded has risen dramatically in the past decade it is still a fraction of one per cent of the school population. It is therefore argued that while home circumstances and family background do have some influence on behavioural responses of young people, there are a whole series of other factors which will also influence their reactions.

The responses of pupils to the questions about their family were scored and frequencies by cumulative percentage were calculated for each phase. The results are summarized in Figure 3.2. The summary scores were calculated from each pupil's return relating to the family, with the lowest scores reflecting a positive perception. The returns of the primary and secondary school pupils are very similar but the returns from the 'special' pupils again suggest a much lower perception of family relationships. Again it may be suggested that these results emphasize the importance of the family influences on the behaviour of the adolescent. However, the story, as can be seen below, becomes more complicated.

Pupils' view – attitude to school

The primary pupils proved to be the most content with their educational provision. Nearly 80 per cent found their lessons to be interesting, compared with 60 per cent of secondary pupils. Also primary pupils were more inclined to feel that their teachers genuinely cared about them as individuals.

Both primary and secondary pupils acknowledged the need for rules and regulations- over 90 per cent in each case considered them to be essential. General confidence (82 per cent primary and 75 per cent of secondary) was expressed about the teachers ability to administer the rules fairly, without picking on individual pupils. This was reflected in the pupils'

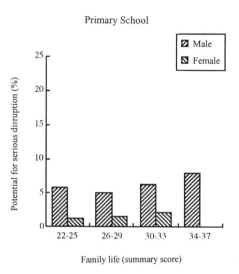

Primary School

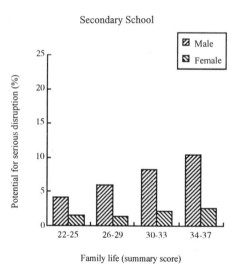

Secondary School

Figure 3.2: Relationship between pupil potential for serious disruption and factors related to the family. Summary scores: Answers to questions were scored, and then for each pupil a total score by section of the questionnaire (see Appendix B) was calculated.

belief that they were told off only when it was deserved (86 per cent primary and 77 per cent of secondary pupils).

The greatest difference of opinion amongst the pupils appeared to be the place of the school uniform. In both sectors pupils were almost evenly split about its virtue – 55 per cent of primary pupils in favour compared with 49 per cent in secondary. However, perhaps the most telling question overall was if the pupils wished they had gone to a different school. Of the total return only 7 per cent would have wished to attend a different school, and with no appreciable difference between the returns of primary and secondary pupils.

Pupils in mainstream schools appeared to readily accept the need of a code of conduct in the school, supported by rules and regulations. There was some dissatisfaction amongst secondary pupils about the quality and vitality of their lessons, coupled with a desire for teachers to show more interest in them as individuals – a point which was subsequently referred to in the most appreciated attributes a teacher may display.

Perhaps understandably, the response from excluded pupils was different – 50 per cent were happy with their existing school, 50 per cent found lessons boring and only 10 per cent saw any virtue in school uniforms. Interestingly, 90 per cent saw the need for school rules and regulations, and in spite of the responses in interviews the majority felt that teachers were fair and caring – perhaps a reflection on the special provision, not their experience of mainstream schools!

The responses of pupils to all of the questions in Section 13 (see Appendix B) of the questionnaire were scored in a similar way to those relating to the family. Section 13 considers three aspects of pupil perception relating to self, school and teachers. These three aspects of pupil perception are shown in the next six histograms which distinguish between the responses of girls and boys at each mainstream phase. In interpreting the graphs it is important to note that the score level relates inversely to the level of perception. Thus a low score reflects a high perception for that particular aspect.

Figure 3.3 examines the perception of self and suggests an increasing propensity for disruption amongst primary school boys and girls with decreasing self-perception. A similar pattern is evident amongst the secondary pupils with the exception of score range 18–21. The importance of self-perception is considered in more detail in Section 15 of the questionnaire (see Appendix B).

Figures 3.4 and 3.5 relating to pupil perception of school and teachers respectively reflect a similar pattern of generally reduced perceptions of the school and the teachers being associated with an increased potential of the pupils for serious disruption. However, the variations in the responses of primary school boys and girls to their school was relatively small. More pronounced is the pupils' responses to their perception of the teacher. For both primary and secondary school pupils there is an increasing tendency towards serious disruption where the pupils' perception of the teacher is of a lower order.

In terms of pupils' self-concept (Section 15 of the questionnaire), the personal, social and academic self-concepts of pupils were scored against the pupils' potential for disruption. The general pattern, with some exceptions reflected that for self-perception i.e. low self-concept related to increased propensity for disruption. Figure 3.6 outlines the personal self-concept summary scores and particularly for secondary school boys suggests a close relationship between personal self-concept and their risk of being involved in acts of disruption. The same is true for secondary boys and their social self-concept scores (Figure 3.7). For other groups the results are apparently much more variable. The most evident pattern of increased risk of pupil involvement in disruption is shown in Figure 3.8 with the parameter of academic self-concept. The patterns of relationship between pupil potential for disruption and the various aspects of self-perception and self-concept as discussed above, though interesting, are of themselves inconclusive. Consequently two further methods of analysis were undertaken.

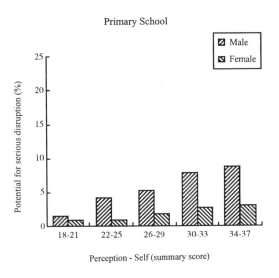

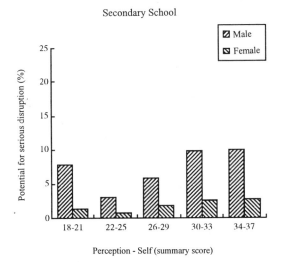

Figure 3.3: Relationship between pupil self-perception and their potential for serious disruption. Summary scores: Answers to questions were scored and then for each pupil a total score by section of the questionnaire (see Appendix B) was calculated.

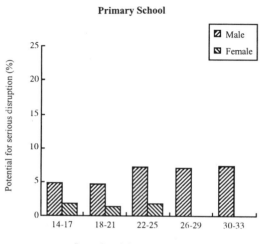

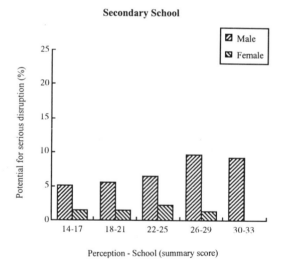

Figure 3.4: Relationship between pupils' perception of school and their potential for serious disruption. Summary scores: Answers to questions were scored and then for each pupil a total score by section of the questionnaire (see Appendix B) was calculated.

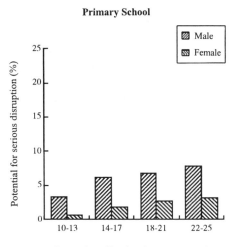

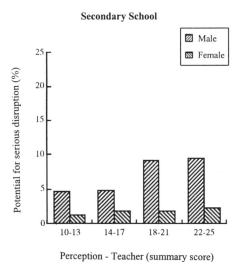

Figure 3.5: Relationship between pupils' perception of their teachers and pupils' potential for serious disruption.
Summary scores: Answers to questions were scored
and then for each pupil a total score by section of the
questionnaire (see Appendix B) was calculated.

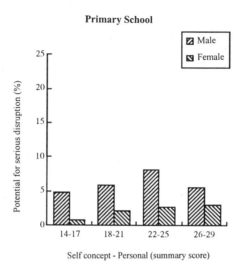

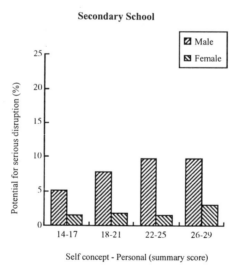

Figure 3.6: Relationship between pupils' personal self-concept and their potential for serious disruption. Summary scores: Answers to questions were scored and then for each pupil a total score by section of the questionnaire (see Appendix B) was calculated.

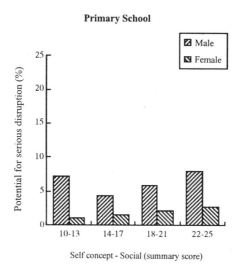

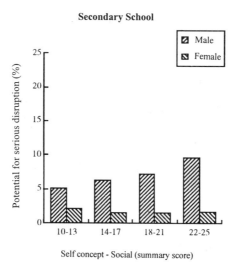

Figure 3.7: Relationship between pupils' social self-concept and their potential for serious disruption. Summary scores: Answers to questions were scored and then for each pupil a total score by section of the questionnaire (see Appendix B) was calculated.

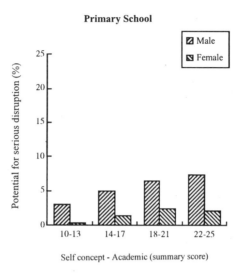

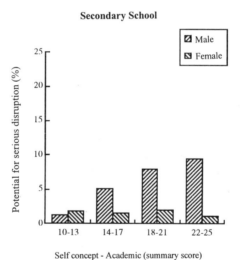

Figure 3.8: Relationship between pupils' academic self-concept and their potential for serious disruption. Summary scores: Answers to questions were scored and then for each pupil a total score by section of the questionnaire (see Appendix B) was calculated.

First, the relationship between pupil potential for disruption and pupil ability level was considered (shown in Figure 3.9), with a self-evident pattern of increased risk of low ability pupils being involved with disruption.

Secondly, pupil responses to the questions in Sections 13 (pupil perception) and 15 (pupil self-concept) of the questionnaire were scored for each phase and the percentage cumulative frequency against the score values were calculated. The main themes from this analysis are:

- Excluded pupils generally have poorer perceptions of their own academic, social and personal self-concepts than mainstream pupils.
- Excluded pupils have poorer perceptions of schools than mainstream pupils, but better perceptions of their teachers (within the special sector).
- Primary school pupils showed closer affiliation and appreciation of their school and teachers than secondary school pupils.
- Primary school pupils had markedly better academic self-concept than their secondary counterparts.
- Generally, secondary school pupils had better social self-concept.

The scores for each pupil correlated against pupil behaviour are summarized in Appendix C. The results, particularly for boys, reflect a close relationship between propensity for disruption and low scores relating to several of the parameters. Perception of the family has a close relationship with behaviour of both primary and secondary school boys. Although the significance of the relationship is high at both phases its dominance appears to diminish at the secondary stage. Similarly the boys' perception of their school and their teachers is closely related to their propensity for disruption. The same is true for primary school girls. Negative self-concept is closely related to primary pupils and secondary boys potential for disruption. For secondary girls

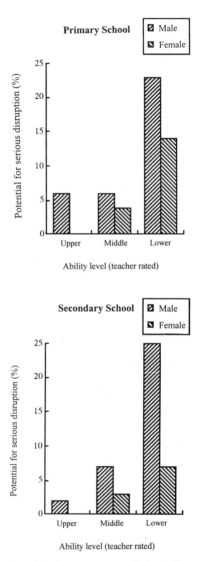

Figure 3.9: Relationship between pupils' ability levels and their potential for serious disruption.

the only parameter with a meaningful relationship with behaviour is personal self-concept.

Pupils' view: attributes of teachers

The open question asked of all pupils in the Scottish study was to name three attributes of teachers that they liked and three that they disliked. Few pupils provided six responses, but each was recorded and given equal weighting. Their responses were placed into one of eight categories and a summary of their return is shown below.

Preferred attributes of teachers.

Characteristic	Primary	Secondary	Special	Total
1. Teaching ability	1085	1351	3	2439
2. Empathy	1028	1066	10	2104
3. Class control	1006	1008	11	2025
4. Personality	1023	945	8	1976
5. Voice	595	330	2	927
6. Type of work	239	199	–	438
7. Privileges	200	68	2	270
8. Other	107	34	–	141

Four significant characteristics were identified as attributes of a 'good' teacher – teaching ability, empathy, class control and personality. Mainstream pupils, particularly secondary, identified teaching ability as their priority attribute of a teacher. The references to teaching ability included clear explanations, interesting topics, regular and supportive marking. The second most preferred quality was empathy for the pupil – a desire expressed as teachers being easy to speak to and demonstrating a readiness to listen to the pupil's point of view. This was not necessarily seen as the teacher always agreeing with them but a demonstration of sensitivity to the pupil as an individual and their perception –

a recognition that children are people. Class control was seen as a further key to good teaching which naturally may be aligned to teaching ability. A well-prepared, well-managed lesson on an interesting topic is much less likely to encourage pupils to misbehave. The fourth major characteristic of the 'good' teacher, personality, referred mainly to their disposition – were they happy and good-humoured people and was this reflected in lessons with a good rapport and an interest in pupils.

Although not in the 'big four', voice was seen as quite important by pupils. The contrast between the sleep-inducing monotone and a range of pace, intonation and accent was referred to. It may be appropriate to place such factors in the category of teaching ability but pupils identified voice separately as a significant feature of good teaching. The other two minor characteristics, type of work and privileges, related to a preference for a practical and investigative style of learning, and to an abhorrence of the use of privileges to 'bribe' pupils to work. The most poignant feature overall was the predominant desire of excluded pupils to have teachers with good class control and friendly personalities – teaching ability was apparently of low significance.

Pupils' view – worst punishment

Pupils were asked what in their view was the worst punishment that a headteacher may inflict. No direction was given and only one answer was accepted. The table below summarizes the responses.

Clearly primary and secondary school pupils perceive exclusion as the ultimate sanction. They also, particularly at primary phase, have some regard for the involvement of parents. The exclusion process and the more positive approach to poor pupil behaviour through the Code of Practice demand early consultation with the parents. Liaison with parents

Type of punishment	Primary	Secondary	Special	Total
1. Exclusion	680	921	5	1606
2. Parental involvement	357	82	–	439
3. Lines	326	24	–	350
4. Detention	143	138	2	283
5. Corporal	36	6	2	48
6. Other	98	18	–	116

provides opportunities to impact positively on the disruptive behaviour of pupils.

Pupils' view – summary

The responses of pupils to the various questions on the questionnaire were related to the pupils' propensity for disruption using a chi-square test. The results are summarized in Appendix D. Individual correlations which are of significance have been highlighted. The main themes are:

- Almost two-thirds of the significant correlations are for boys.
- Generally, both primary and secondary school pupils have a good perception of their family but those pupils who perceive their family relationships relatively poorly are more likely to be designated as potentially disruptive.
- Primary pupils held their teachers and their school in higher esteem than the secondary pupils, and particularly so for the pupils who are deemed potentially disruptive.
- Primary school pupils have higher personal and academic self-concepts, and lower social self-concept, than secondary school pupils.
- Pupils, particularly boys, with low self-perception and low self-concept are more prone to disruption.
- Pupils with low academic ability are at greater risk of being involved with incidents of disruption.

The outcome from studying the responses of these 3000 pupils is that pupil perception and self-esteem are closely associated with pupil behaviour. Poor self-esteem increases the likelihood of adverse and inappropriate behaviour in school. The level of self-esteem is related to many factors, including school and home circumstances. The role of these parameters, amongst other considerations, are discussed in the next two chapters.

Bibliography

Coleman, J S (1966) *Equality of Educational Opportunity.* U.S. Government Printing Office.

Coleman, J C and Hendry, L B (1990) *The Nature of Adolescence.* Routledge.

Craft, M, Raynor, J and Cohen, L (1980) *Linking Home and School.* Harper and Row.

DFE (1994) *Code of Practice on the Identification and Assessment of Special Educational Need.* Welsh Office.

Docking, J W (1980) *Control and Discipline in Schools.* Wheaton.

Docking, J W (1989) In *School Management and Pupil Behaviour.* Falmer.

Epstein, S (1973) The self-concept revisited or a theory of a theory. *American Psychologist,* 28.

Fitts, W A and Hammer, W (1969) *The Self-Concept and Delinquency.* Research Monograph 1 CAIO 74.

Harter, S (1983) *The Development of the Self-system.* Wiley.

Heath, A and Clifford, P (1980) *The Seventy Thousand Hours Rutter Left Out.* Oxford Review of Education (Volume 6, No. 2).

Jones, R A (1977) *Self-fulfilling Prophesies.* Lawrence Erlbaum Associates.

Lawrence, J, Steed, D and Young, P (1984) *Disruptive Children – Disruptive Schools.* Croom Helm.

McCail, G (1981) *Mother Start.* SCRE.

Reid, K (1986) *Disaffection from School.* Methuen.

Rosenberg, M (1979) *Conceiving the Self.* New York: Basic Books.

Ruddock, J, Chaplain, R and Wallace, G (1996) *School Improvement: What Can Pupils Tell Us?* David Fulton Publishers.

Sanders, D (1990) *The Class Struggle.* Unpublished PhD Thesis.

Tizard, B and Hughes, M (1984) *Young Children Learning.* Fontana.

Watt, J and Flett, M (1985) *Continuity in Early Education.* Department of Education, Aberdeen University.

4   Perspectives on pupil behaviour in schools

NEWS HEADLINES

SCHOOLBOYS TERRORIZE THE NEIGHBOURHOOD (A)

BOYS OCCUPY COLLEGE BUILDINGS (B)

PUPIL REVOLUTION – REGULAR TROOPS SENT IN (C)

WOMAN TEACHER THREATENED (D)

PUPIL STABBED (E)

ATTACKS BY PUPILS ON TEACHERS ARE INCREASING (F)

STAFF DEMAND SUPPORT OVER PUPIL ATTACKS (G)

These headline stories provide a picture of the behaviour of some pupils and the disruptive incidents in which they were involved. Do they shock or surprise the reader? We think not. Do they reflect news items which you have read in the news-paper or seen on the television recently? The headlines (A), (B) and (C), although made up by the authors, do refer to real incidents which took place in the sixteenth and seventeenth centuries at renowned public schools. (D) and (E) were adapted from Lowndes (1969) and are potential headlines of incidents which took place in the early 1900s. The last two headlines are more recent. (F) is taken from Crequer's report in the *Independent* (9.4.88) and (G) was reported in the *Independent* on 2.2.96 by Fran Abrams.

Agressive and disruptive behaviour is not a new phenomenon, but one which has been evident from the first days of formalized schooling. It would be equally as inappropriate to judge the quality of education and standards of behaviour in the past from a few documented and sensationalized incidents, as it would be today. Equally it would be foolish to ignore them. If we consider 'headline' (F), it reflects many media reports of deteriorating standards of pupil behaviour in schools. This was also seen in the literature of the 1980s (Lawrence *et al.*, 1984; Gilmore *et al.*, 1985; Reid, 1986). The contemporary alternative view was provided by Wheldall and Merrett (1988) and Wragg (1988) whose research suggested that only a very small percentage of teachers had difficulty with discipline and that it was the relatively minor but more frequently occurring (and thereby most irritating) acts of misbehaviour that caused most damage to the quality of pupils' learning, such as 'TOOT' – talking out of turn. But does talking out of turn constitute disruption? Surely the act of disruption needs to be more violent if it is to be considered disruptive – or perhaps it needs to happen very frequently? Let us attempt a closer definition of disruption.

Towards a definition of disruption

Is there a natural (and perhaps deemed healthy) tendency for pupils to misbehave? In schools the opportunity for such behaviour will vary from teacher to teacher and according to different situations – such as the different opportunity available between normal lesson times and unsupervised sessions such as breaks and lunchtimes. The variation between misbehaving and what is considered disruptive is very fine. Who makes such a judgement and does it apply to the incident or the pupils involved? It is easy to apply the term 'disruptive' to an incident or a situation. The complication comes when it is used in relation to a pupil, that is, a 'disruptive' pupil. It may be argued that any pupil involved in an incident of disruption, at least at that time, is disruptive. However, is it appropriate to use the term 'disruptive' more generally about a pupil if he or she has been involved in only one such incident? Perhaps two, or three or four incidents of disruption should result in a pupil being classified as 'disruptive'. It is natural and indeed 'childlike' for pupils to be mischievous and to be disruptive on occasions. For as Reid (1986) reminds us, 'teachers need to remember that it is quite natural for all pupils to misbehave occasionally, as most pupils will testify'.

If we do not accept this assumption then it means that virtually all pupils can be regarded as disruptive ,i.e. the 'normal' child is disruptive. If we regard low levels of misbehaviour as being normal, as Reid (1986) suggests, then establishing the level at which the pupil's misbehaviour is to be considered abnormal becomes extremely difficult. Should the level be set by the number of incidents of misbehaviour, by the frequency of such incidents, or by the degree of misbehaviour? If so, what should be the yardstick to measure the number, frequency or intensity of such incidents? Even if such a boundary could be established it would be highly subjective and of limited use in classifying pupils and of no use in aiding our understanding of the difficulties experienced by the pupil.

The 'Pupils with Problems' circulars from DFE (1994) are more definitive and prescriptive than any other preceding regulations on identifying and providing for pupils with emotional and behavioural difficulties. They include the nature of behaviours which may lead to exclusion and indeed those which should not. However, there is no absolute definitive level of adverse behaviour in either type or frequency which is identified as leading to an exclusion. These are deemed matters for professional judgement at a local level.

Coulby and Harper's (1985) contribution is to use the term 'disruption' to describe the nature of incidents and not to use it to describe pupils. They suggest that classifying incidents rather than pupils removes the stigma from the pupil and in turn this will help to create a more positive climate through which beneficial behavioural change can be effected. Cooper *et al.* (1994) extend this argument into an 'ecosystemic' approach in which emphasis is placed on the impact of social interactions.

The main idea is that human beings are social beings, who are as dependent on the social environment for their mental well-being, as they are on the physical environment for their survival. According to this view, human beings are neither wholly free, in an existential sense, to behave as they choose, nor is their behaviour wholly determined by environmental forces. Human beings exist within a social web, rather like a biological ecosystem in which the individual's behaviour and development of others with whom s/he interacts. From an ecosystemic viewpoint, human behaviour is the product of ongoing interaction between influences in the social environment and internal motivations which derive from prior (mainly social) experience. Furthermore, the overarching, twin human needs for a recognized personal identity and a sense of social belonging make the social group (or system) the central focus of human activity, to the extent that individuals' personal needs and motivations are often subordinate to the group as a whole. The potential for conflict, both interpersonal and intrapersonal, in such circumstances is obvious. All group members depend upon the group to supply particular needs thus the maintenance of the group is paramount, even if its maintenance requires the sacrifice of one of its members

(Cooper *et al.*, 1994)

Cooper *et al.* (1994) and Coulby and Harper (1985) approach acts of disruption with great understanding from a pupil perspective, trying to acknowledge and take cognisance of the complexity of what is taking place and deflecting the 'blame' which may be left with the pupils directly involved in the act of disruption. Nevertheless some pupils are more prone to being involved in incidents of misbehaviour than others and some are more prone to being involved in incidents of a serious nature. The nature of the incident or the forms of behaviour which may be classified as disruptive are infinite. However, broadly speaking they can be divided into two categories of acts of disruption – serious incidents which require consideration of immediate exclusion of pupils involved, or less serious but frequently recurring patterns of disruption which are irritating and thereby impede the process of learning.

Types of disruption

Serious acts of disruption include the most extreme forms of behaviour such as grievous assault and rape. Similarly drug pushing and extortion may fall into the category of 'serious' act of disruption and further may lead to legal action being taken. Clearly in such cases when adolescents have been successfully prosecuted there would be a change in terminology of the nature of the incident from an act of disruption to one of delinquency. Fortunately even today the frequency in schools of such incidents nationally is relatively rare (Wheldall and Merrett, 1988, 1992; Docking, 1980; Sanders, 1990; HMCI, 1996). Sanders comments that while headteachers found dealing with such serious incidents of disruption traumatic at the time of the incident, the follow-up was relatively straightforward because there was rarely any dubiety among the supporting agencies as to the seriousness of the incident or the type of provision which would best meet the pupil's needs. In terms of exclusions these are the types of incidents which, regardless of the pupil's track record, are commonly agreed to be so serious that, in order to protect both the staff and the pupils within the school, permanent exclusion of the offending pupil is an essential prerequisite.

The second type of disruption includes all of the minor incidents and acts of misbehaviour which teachers have to contend with every day. Wheldall and Merrett (1988) and Sanders (1990) demonstrated that teachers often found much less serious forms of disruption more difficult because of the much greater frequency – sometimes a near-constant source of irritation. Wheldall and Merrett, for example, in their survey of secondary school teacher responses to the most troublesome behaviour, discovered that the overwhelming majority found pupils 'talking out of turn' to be the most irritating and educationally most damaging for the class as a whole. But how many times does a pupil need to talk out of turn before the draconian measure of exclusion is considered?

Thus disruptive behaviour includes these relatively minor forms of misbehaviour at the lower end of the scale and the very serious incidents bordering on the criminal at the top end. Clearly the term disruption has become an umbrella term and lacks precise definition. Equally there are a number of other terms used to describe anti-social behaviour, such as deviant, maladaptive and maladjusted, but these also lack precise definitions.

> ... there is no point at which 'maladjustment' suddenly begins or ends
>
> (Blackham, 1967)

Many researchers have tried to define a more precise definition of disruption, particularly as it applies to schools, e.g.

- Lowenstein (1975): any behaviour, short of physical violence which interferes with the teaching process and/or upsets the normal running of the school
- Lawrence (1981): any behaviour which seriously interferes with the teaching process and/or seriously upsets the normal

running of the school. It is more than misbehaviour ... and includes physical attacks and malicious damage to property

- Galloway (1982): disruptive behaviour is any behaviour which appears problematic, inappropriate and disturbing to teachers
- Sanders (1990): disruptive behaviour is any behaviour which is detrimental to order and discipline in the school or the educational well-being of the pupils there (Associated with the Scottish School General Regulations 1982)

None of these commentaries provide a precise definition of disruption and perhaps in relation to the term 'disruption' we should leave the last word to Topping (1983) who argues that 'like intelligence, "disruptive" is a loose, vernacular word and serves its function best by so remaining providing this is understood'.

It is evident that without the possibility of a precise definition of the term disruptive, it is impossible to measure the level of disruption in schools and compare rates of disruption from school to school or from authority to authority. Establishing criteria to identify the number or nature of acts of disruption necessary to warrant an exclusion is equally difficult. Therefore such decisions do have to be left to the professional judgement of senior staff in the schools (DFE Circular 10/94). But once a pupil has been permanently excluded, can they then be appropriately described as 'disruptive'? As the majority of pupils who fall into this category are 15 years of age and by definition will have been involved in serious incidents of disruption, or conducted minor acts of disruption frequently over a sustained period, surely the answer has to be yes. Pupils who have been excluded, and particularly those who have been permanently excluded, must be considered to have at least a higher incidence of involvement in acts of serious disruption than their peers and therefore be eligible for the title 'disruptive pupil'.

Disruption to permanent exclusion

As there are no universal indicators of disruption, exclusion may be regarded as a means of objectively reflecting the amount of poor behaviour in schools today. While temporary exclusions may be used quite appropriately in different ways within school sanction and discipline policies, the act of permanent exclusion 'should be used as a last resort, when all other reasonable steps have been taken, and when allowing the child to remain in school would be seriously detrimental to the education or welfare of the pupil or of others' (DFE 10/94). The interpretation of these criteria will vary but all headteachers are obliged to operate within the constraint of the guidance and require the ratification of permanent exclusions by the Governors and additionally, for maintained schools, the LEA. These processes should bring some standardization to the record of pupils who have been permanently excluded. The numbers of pupils who have been permanently excluded have been recorded through NERS (National Exclusions Reporting System) since 1990/91. The first two years of reporting reflected similar pictures of the number and nature of exclusions in England and Wales:

- Three thousand permanent exclusions take place annually.
- Only 13 per cent of the total number of pupils are from primary schools.
- Four boys are excluded for every girl.
- The modal age for exclusion is 15.
- The main factors leading to exclusion include constantly refusing to obey school rules, verbal abuse or insolence.
- The incidence of physical aggression accounted for 27 per cent of the permanent exclusions (percentage against – teachers (7), other staff (1), pupils(19)).
- Variations in the number of exclusions are too great to be explained by socio-economic factors of a school's catchment area.

The DFE commissioned Canterbury Christ Church College to undertake a 'National survey of local authorities' policies and procedures for the identification of, and provision for, children who are out of school by reason of exclusion or otherwise. The report of the study was published in July 1995. The national survey was repeated for 1995/6 and the number of permanent exclusions from each phase is summarized below (Table 4.1).

Table 4.1: Pupils permanently excluded from maintained schools in England in the period 1 September 1995 – 31 July 1996.

Phase	Boys	Girls	Total for 91 LEAs	Total for 117 LEAs	Percentages (%)
Primary	1414	99	1513	1872	13.7
Secondary	7346	1619	9037	11159	82.17
Special	397	52	449	550	4.05
Overall total			10999	13581	100

Source: Final report on the follow-up survey of permanent exclusions from schools in England – 1995/96.

The difference between the rate of exclusion in primary and secondary schools is quite striking. The reasons for such differences are manifold but include the significant variation in the regime of the two phases, the timetabling and staffing differences, the impact of adolescence both physically and emotionally on secondary school pupils. There is also a perceived response of primary schools wanting to 'cope' with the whole of their population, and contain difficult pupils. Their noble efforts to maintain pupils in mainstream schools do not necessarily extend to the secondary phase. However, it may be argued that for many of these pupils the signs of disaffection were already evident and that the coping strategy did little to meet pupils' needs. The 1993 Education Act and the requirements of the Code of Practice (DFE, 1994) will help in the earlier identification of pupils with special needs and more appropriate educational planning to meet their needs (see Chapter 5). The other stark contrast is between the relatively high number of boys permanently excluded compared with the girls.

The picture in England and Wales is one of an increasing use of permanent exclusion. However, the detailed analysis of this data is yet to be undertaken. In Scotland similar approaches to reviewing the exclusion record were commissioned in 1987. MacPhee (1987) surveyed the Scottish Authorities about policies on exclusion, their value for individual pupils and for the school as a whole. His view was that the approach of each authority was so different that effective comparison was not possible. However, he suggested that the variation evident from the number of exclusions from authority to authority was also evident from school to school. Consequently he argued that the differences of the exclusion record across Scotland owe as much to responses at school level as they do to variations of policy at authority level.

However, MacPhee (1987), following a programme of research similar to that of Parsons (1995), reviewed the levels of exclusion for one year only. Recent research conducted by Her Majesty's Inspectors of Schools (HMI) also confined their study to data related to exclusions, and associated factors, from one academic year only – 1994/5 (HMCI, 1996). The question emerges as to whether or not premises which are based on the exclusion record of schools over one academic year hold through time. If the data of schools is considered over several years, does a pattern of exclusion develop which supports the hypothesis that the level of exclusion is almost entirely related to school-based factors? The Scottish study undertaken by the authors attempted to overcome the limitations of using the data from one year only by reviewing the record of exclusion of fifteen secondary schools over a period of seven years.

Exclusion patterns from fifteen secondary schools in a large Scottish city

Naturally the exclusion policy which applied to all fifteen schools reflected national requirements. Additionally it also required headteachers to try all measures available to support difficult pupils and placed emphasis on early intervention.

> ... all internal preventive and remedial procedures should have been exhausted. Learning difficulties, medical factors, poor attainment, excessive demands and like matters should have been considered and required action taken.
>
> (Authority Policy Statement)

Once all other internal measures had broken down, and it should be noted that these internal measures required parental involvement, the headteacher may proceed to exclusion. The policy included three types of exclusion: two were short term and were issued by the headteacher and the third, a 'sine die' or permanent exclusion, could only be sanctioned by the Divisional Education Officer. Clearly the process of permanent exclusion suggested that there had been an irretrievable breakdown at the child's school but completion of the exclusion could only be approved by an officer external to the school.

The underpinning philosophy of the short-term exclusions was reported to be multi-purpose in so far as they provided a sanction for the school: a 'cooling off' period for both the pupil and the school; a warning to the pupil, to the effect that further acts of disruption may lead to permanent exclusion; and a means of establishing conditions of a pupil's return to school that are designed to aid their continuation in the local school. Even so, the three types of exclusion were not always used sequentially.

The exclusion rate of the fifteen schools is summarized in the graph shown in Figure 4.1. Exclusion rates would, for any

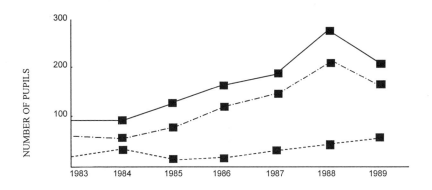

YEAR DATE INDICATES END OF SESSION

i.e. 1983 INDICATES END OF 1982/3

KEY

TOTAL NUMBER OF EXCLUSIONS

SHORT TERM EXCLUSIONS (RETURN TO HOME SCHOOL)

'SINE DIE' EXCLUSIONS

Figure 4.1: Graph showing the exclusion pattern of pupils from schools in a major Scottish city from 1983 to 1989.

one year, suggest that exclusions are hugely variable and knowledge of the area would confirm that these variations are not specific to the type of catchment area. The conclusion drawn must be that the rate of exclusion relates strongly with school regime. However, if the levels of exclusion for the same schools are considered over several years, the picture is far more complex, with schools showing significant fluctuation of the number of exclusions through time (see Table 4.2). Consequently it would be argued that much of the analysis related to the level of exclusion for individual schools is flawed, because it is not taken over a sufficient period of time.

Three approaches to the analysis of the record of exclusion have been undertaken. First, the overall trend of the total number of exclusions from all schools from 1983 to 1989 are considered (see Figure 4.1). Secondly, the rates of exclusion from each of the fifteen secondary schools are examined over a six-year period (see Table 4.2). [Secondary schools were selected for this exercise because they most commonly excluded pupils and thereby created the most consistent record of exclusion through time.] Thirdly, some measure of the success of exclusions are considered.

The main outcome of these three forms of analysis are summarized below:

- The rate of exclusion increased significantly over the period of seven years.
- Boys are much more prone to exclusion than girls.
- The number of exclusions from each secondary school irrespective of catchment area and management, fluctuate annually.
- Short-term exclusion is used increasingly as a school sanction.
- Approximately 80 per cent of pupils excluded short term are not excluded permanently.
- Headteachers found exclusion to be a suitable sanction which 'protected' the school.
- Permanent exclusion did not automatically result in pupils being transferred to alternative provision.

Table 4.2: Number of exclusions from secondary schools in a large Scottish city during the period 1983 to 1988.

| School | Year | | | | | |
	1983	1984	1985	1986	1987	1988
School A	7	7	10	16	15	27
School B*	10	8	19	14	6	16
School C	6	6	8	6	6	14
School D	1	1	0	2	1	1
School E	1	1	0	10	17	19
School F*	11	9	6	7	22	24
School G	5	6	6	4	8	12
School H	6	7	20	17	6	13
School J*	3	4	8	13	27	16
School K	0	2	7	8	3	3
School L*	1	1	5	6	0	6
School M	17	12	12	21	31	19
School N	1	2	1	3	16	36
School P*	9	5	5	5	13	22
School R*	1	7	4	2	7	30

*Six most stable schools in relation to the school regime.

Note that for the six most stable school regimes (marked *) there are significant variations ($\chi^2(25) = 77.98$, P < 0.0001) in the number of exclusions by year.

Scottish study – increasing rate of exclusion 1983–89

Table 4.3 shows the raw total figures of exclusion and illustrate the increasing trend for pupils to be excluded during the seven-year period. The figures show total numbers of permanent (sine die) exclusions for the years 1983 to 1989. In Figure 4.1 the total number of exclusions throughout this period is dominated by the short-term exclusions and consequently

Table 4.3: Ratio of permanent exclusions to the total pupil roll in a large Scottish city during the period 1983 to 1989.

	Year						
	1983	1984	1985	1986	1987	1988	1989
(1) Total no. of exclusions	90	89	120	162	189	287	248
(2) Total schools' pop'n (×100)	330	325	314	308	303	297	293
(3) Ratio (1) to (2) = 1 to ...	367	365	262	192	160	103	118
(4) Total no. 'sine die' exclusions	29	36	34	36	49	58	60
(5) 'Sine die' exclusions as % of total school pop'n	0.09	0.11	0.11	0.12	0.16	0.20	0.20

the curves on the graph representing these figures are nearly parallel. The gradients of these curves from 1984 to 1987 are fairly uniform, rising sharply from 1987 to 1988 and falling back in 1989. By contrast, the line indicating the number of 'sine die' exclusions shows a much more constant gradient and does not reflect such a significant upward trend from 1987 to 1988. The pattern of change over the six-year period shown might be summarized as one in which the exclusion rate has more than tripled, and of which an increasingly large majority come from the short-term exclusion category.

If these figures are contrasted with the total pupil numbers over the same time period, then it would be seen that the increase in exclusion was against a background of reducing roll (see Table 4.3). For example, in 1983 the ratio of excluded pupils to non-excluded pupils was 1:367 and this contrasted with 1:103 in 1988, and 1:118 in 1989. On a pro rata basis the rate of exclusion has increased during this period by over 350 per cent. This extremely rapid increase was not matched by the increased rate of 'sine die' exclusion of 0.9 per thousand in 1983 compared with 2.0 per thousand in 1989. Clearly, in both absolute and percentage terms the increase in the number of exclusions is quite dramatic, particularly from 1987 to 1988.

The annual exclusion figure for each individual secondary school is tabulated in Table 4.2, in which schools have been randomized and lettered so they may remain anonymous. The total number of exclusions annually in the period 1983–89 shows an upward trend (see Figure 4.1), as do the figures for secondary schools. However, none of the secondary schools shows a steady and continual increase in the numbers of ex-clusions experienced. The pattern for most of the schools shows a whole series of peaks and troughs during the course of the six-year period (see Table 4.2). For example, school J shows five years of continuous increase, followed by a re-duction in 1988 at which time the general trend was very sig-nificantly upwards. In 1987, school J reached its peak with 27 permanent exclusions which placed it fourteenth in the league table but this fell dramatically the following year with sixteen exclusions, re-establishing it in seventh place in the hierarchy. Similar fluctuations of the absolute numbers of exclusions and the school's position in a hierarchy apply to the majority of the schools listed. The significant change in total figures of exclusions from 1987 to 1988 (see Figure 4.1) reflects an increase of some 50 per cent and this level of change is to be seen in seven of the fifteen schools. In sharp contrast the remaining eight schools show a marginal increase, a maintenance of the status quo or a dramatic fall. In other words, the general trend of significant increase masks a whole range of changes which were taking place in individual schools. Similarly, it can be seen that not only does the annual pattern show remarkable variation, but each individual school reflects fluctuation.

Although the general upward trend can perhaps be ac-coun-ted for through one of many factors at the time such as the effects of industrial action, general societal change in attitude to authority, withdrawal of corporal punishment and increased familiarity with exclusion procedure, it is much more difficult to explain the massive annual variations in exclusions returns within an individual school. The possible causes of such dramatic changes in the figures may be a product of: (a) a change in the members of staff, particularly senior members of staff; (b) adjustments to pastoral care and discipline policies; (c) changes in accommodation; (d) the influence of the Parents' Charter on the roll of a school; (e) any changes in parental/community involvement; and (f) of course, changes in curricular policy. In order for the potential influence of these factors to be reduced to a minimum, six of the fifteen schools were selected for further analysis.

These six schools were selected on the basis of being most stable in terms of staffing and organization, over the period 1983 to 1989. These schools did not have major changes of staffing and particularly not at senior management level. Equally, the school population, both from within and out of zone, remained consistent and none of the schools had major changes in accommodation or facilities.

However, if we consider Figure 4.2 in which the exclusion numbers for each of the six schools are shown graphically, it can be seen that the pattern of exclusion for each school is extremely varied, and illustrates not only significant changes in the gradients of the curve but massive swings from positive to negative and negative to positive. The only trend that would appear to be shown by the vast majority, is that of a significant increase in the exclusion figures from 1987 to 1988. The fluctuations of the graphs throughout the rest of the period suggest the results are random. It is the very random nature of the graphs that weakens any suggestion that there is
a causal relationship between the exclusion figures and the school regime.

Further, for the six selected schools, consideration was given to establishing causal relationships between the school and the catchment area. Although there has not been a detailed socio-economic analysis of these areas, the schools could be described as falling into one of three categories:

- Predominantly private housing (schools L and P).
- Schools with a fairly equal mix of private and rented properties (schools R and B).
- Schools with predominantly rented accommodation (schools F and J).

This categorization of the socio-economic areas is reflected by the returns indicating the predominant occupations of each area in the pupil questionnaire returns.

Conventional wisdom leads us to believe that the better the socio-economic area, the fewer the discipline problems, resulting in a lower number of exclusions. Close consideration of Figure 4.2 would show this to be only partly true for the six selected schools. Clearly any difference between the exclusion rates of two schools could be a product of different tolerance levels of poor behaviour. However, such a view is not consistent with the evidence of the graphs. The fluctuation of the lines counters suggestions of correlations with parameters which do not change dramatically on an annual basis.

'Success' of exclusions from fifteen secondary schools

School perspective

The general trend of the exclusion during the period 1983–88 was upward but this masks a fairly uniform curve for 'sine die' exclusions, contrasting with a dramatic increase in short-term exclusions (see Figure 4.1). The two curves show remarkably different gradients, indicative of short-term exclusions being used more commonly by schools, and although 'sine die' exclusions show an increase, they were by no means at the same rate. If we take the frequency of

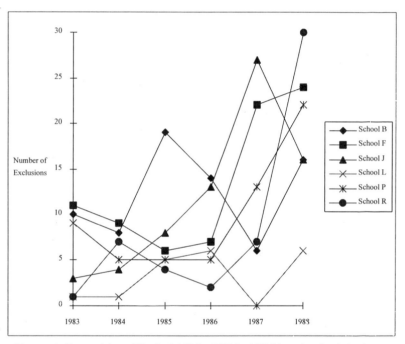

There are significant variations within schools ($\chi^2(25) = 77.98$, P < 0.0001) in number of exclusions by year

Figure 4.2: The exclusion pattern from 1983 to 1988 of six selected secondary schools.

exclusion only, the marked difference in the figure for 1988 suggests that, as an effective sanction, exclusion was losing some of its potency. However, in 1989 there was a downward trend of the total exclusion figures. On the whole, headteachers agreed that judicious use of exclusion procedure was a powerful weapon in the overall sanctions available to schools. Pupils confirmed the 'value' of exclusion in this respect (see Chapter 3).

Pupil reaction

The effectiveness of exclusion can also be measured by the use of the procedure to highlight the needs of pupils and the response to the identification of pupils' needs. The research on exclusions in the Scottish study considers these points in two ways. First, does the system of exclusion result in pupils, parents and other services becoming more aware of a pupil's problems, and secondly, if pupils are highlighted as having special educational needs, is the provision available to provide for a more successful form of schooling? Experience suggests that nothing raises the priority of need of the pupil and ensures inter-agency involvement as much as exclusion, particularly when parents are seeking educational provision for their excluded son/daughter. However, is the process of exclusion and its accompanying distress for both the pupil and parents justified by the ensuing response and subsequent educational provision? There has been little research into the former, but discussion with many headteachers, teachers and psychologists would suggest there to be justification and benefits derived at school level. The research (Grunsell, 1980; Galloway, 1982; McLean, 1986) suggests the majority of excluded pupils are located back in mainstream schools and complete their education there. It could, therefore, be argued at a very simplistic level that for such pupils the act of exclusion had brought their problems to a 'head' and the discussion about the exclusion and following input enabled them to survive in mainstream. In the Scottish study between 80 and 90 percent of the pupils excluded temporarily completed their education at that school, i.e. without being permanently excluded. At this very basic level, such a course of action may be deemed successful. In contrast, those pupils who are located outside mainstream education do not appear to benefit, either academically or socially, from their experience (Topping, 1983; Skinner *et al.*, 1983; Galloway in Cohen and Cohen, 1987).

> On commonsense grounds it might seem surprising if pupils improved after transfer to special school or centres. All teachers and all parents know that children learn from each other. One wonders what they are supposed to learn when placed in a separate school or class with a lot of other pupils presenting similar severe behavioural problems. In this connection it is irrelevant whether the special provision is class operated as part of the school's special education network or a separate school or centre serving the whole LEA
>
> (Galloway in Cohen and Cohen, 1987)

Given that most centres for alternative education would give, as their main aim, the return of pupils to mainstream, the success of such centres is questionable.

> The evidence does not suggest that these schools are frequently successful in returning pupils to the mainstream nor that placement results in any long-term improvements in the pupils' behaviour. (Galloway in Cohen and Cohen, 1987)

Clearly, the research questioned the value of the exclusion procedure as an identifier of pupils who were experiencing difficulties, and further, would question the type of provision that was made once the difficulties of a pupil had been recognized. Tattum (1986) raises a further issue about exclusion procedure and that is the length of time that elapsed before alternative provision was made available to the excluded pupil. Where this was a long period of time, Tattum suggests, pupils are placed at risk and it is highly unlikely that their time will be used constructively. Indeed, pupils may drift into offending, and thus exacerbate their problems – perhaps completing a self-fulfilling prophecy.

The irony of the exclusion record

The starting point for pupils to slide down the slope of exclusion is school. Different schools have different regimes which in turn have helped or hindered youngsters down the slope of exclusion (Rutter *et al.*, 1979; Hargreaves, 1984; Reid, 1986). The differences in the school management regime which affect the potential for exclusion are manifold, and it has been suggested that the exclusion record is a reflection of the quality of the school management and much less a reflection of the catchment area (Rutter *et al.*, 1979; Coulby and Harper, 1985; Lawrence *et al.*, 1984). The results of this study suggest that as exclusion rates vary considerably year by year without variation of the management team/style, other parameters must be at work to affect the rate of exclusion and thereby pupil propensity for disruption.

This is not to suggest that the role of the management team is unimportant but that in spite of stable senior management and similar conditions prevailing, exclusion rates in schools have varied significantly through time. These results add weight to the findings of Chapter 3 which places emphasis on the importance of pupil self-esteem and self-concept and their impact on pupils' predilection for disruption. Nevertheless the authors would share the view that the quality of leadership in schools does strongly influence the standards of pupil behaviour.

> Our evidence indicates universal agreement that the quality of leadership provided by the headteacher and the senior management team (deputies, senior teachers etc.) is crucial to a school's success in promoting good behaviour. Mortimore's study of junior schools found that good work and behaviour were not only linked with purposeful leadership by the headteacher but with active involvement of the deputy head in managing the school. We are aware of many examples both here and in the USA, of schools in difficulty which have been turned around by

energetic heads and senior management teams. The concept of teachers as a team manager even in a small primary school can be a powerful starting point for improvement.

Our visit to schools convinced us that, while good heads can have different personal styles, consistent themes run through effective school management. These include clear aims for teachers and pupils and good staff morale and team work. Effective leadership tends to produce a positive atmosphere and a general sense of security.

(Elton Report, 1989)

The role of the senior management team is not to be underestimated. Taking cognisance of such views, Sanders (1990) endeavoured to seek the opinions of headteachers in both primary and secondary phases. In the Scottish study headteachers' views on the management of disruption in schools were examined. Their responses are considered next.

Headteachers' views on managing disruption

The possibility of the school regime having a 'causal' relationship with the level of disruption has been discussed already. The analysis of the exclusion record suggested that at least for the most extreme forms of disruption, the true picture is more complicated. Schools examined in the Scottish study have a variable exclusion record through time in spite of no other significant changes in the nature of the school. It is believed that this casts some doubt on the over-simplistic view that schools can be judged on the basis of one set of statistics as being either 'good' or 'bad'. What is clear is that headteachers will have a major role in responding to incidents of disruption and their impact may be positive in resolving situations or otherwise.

What are the views of headteachers on handling pupils with behavioural problems? Do they have any preferred method of dealing with incidents? What punishments do they apply and are they effective? In order to gain some insight into these questions, some 65 primary headteachers were asked their views on disruption. The research centred on primary headteachers so that their responses could be related to a relatively small catchment area and therefore be more reflective of the socio-economic character of the neighbourhood which they serve. The headteachers were asked their opinion on: (a) the most common types of disruption; (b) the most difficult types of disruption to cope with; (c) the most effective sanctions; and (d) recommendations to help resolve the problems of disruption. The responses from the headteachers were categorized according to the nature of the catchment area of the school; the size of the school; and the style of the school, that is, whether or not the school was open plan. The relationship between these three parameters and the returns from the headteachers were tested using chi-square.

A. The most common types of disruption

The results of the returns on the most common types of disruption are shown as a hierarchy in Table 4.4. Clearly headteachers felt that fighting was the most common type of disruption, but testing this against the parameters of social class, size and style of the schools did not raise any statistically significant results. This suggested that from the headteachers' perspective there was no evident difference between pupils (comments predominantly referred to boys) of very different home backgrounds predisposition to fighting.

The type of behaviour which created the next most common difficulty for headteachers was that of attention-seeking.

Table 4.4: The most common types of disruption.

Type of dis-ruption	No. of returns	Returns subdivided by							
		Type of housing			Size			Style	
		1	2	3	S	M	L	O	C
1 Fighting	25 Ob	5	7	13	5	8	12	4	21
	Ex	7.6	8.1	9.3	3.2	8.9	12.9	5.2	19.8
2 Attention-seeking	20 Ob	5	8	7	2	7	11	4	16
	Ex	6.1	6.5	7.4	2.6	7.1	10.3	4.2	15.8
3 Not working	17 Ob	5	5	7	1	5	11	6	11
	Ex	5.2	5.5	6.3	2.2	6	8.8	3.6	13.4
4 Disobedience	16 Ob *	2	8	6	2	4	10	5	11
	Ex	4.9	5.2	5.9	2.1	5.7	8.3	3.4	12.6
5 Playground incidents (un-supervised)	10 Ob	1	3	6	1	4	5	1	9
	Ex	3.1	3.2	3.7	1.3	3.5	5.2	2.1	7.9
Sub-totals	Ob	18	31	39	11	28	49	20	68
	Ex	26.9	28.5	32.6	11.4	31.2	45.4	18.5	69.5
6 Others	12	Including theft, lying, tantrums, lateness, peer relations, vandalism							

Legend

Type of housing	Size of school	Style
1 – Mainly owner occupied	S – Small (<120 pupils)	O – Open plan
2 – Good mix of rented/owned property	M – Medium (120–220 pupils)	C – Cellular classes
3 – Mainly rented properties	L – Large (>220 pupils)	

Results: Ob – Observed	Ex – Expected	* (x at 0.05 level of significance)

The relationship between the nature and frequency of attention-seeking behaviour shows a random pattern of distribution. In other words, the social class, the size of the school and the style of the school would appear to have no relationship with the degree of attention-seeking that takes place. A similar, though slightly less marked paralleling of observed and expected results can be seen in the next most common category, 'Not Working'.

Category 4, Disobedience, is the only item in which a statistically significant result was returned and which relates to the social class, as reflected by the housing of the school's catchment area. Interestingly, it was not entirely the pattern that 'conventional wisdom' may have anticipated. Certainly the 'better' housing areas show a significantly lower return on disobedience and, by contrast, schools with a mixed catchment show significantly higher return, but the schools with a catchment which is mainly made up of rented properties have a level of disobedience that is very close to the expected level. There is a danger of reading too much into this result because, first, the level of significance statistically is only at 0.05 and secondly, the definition of disobedience will vary from school to school. The other relationships between disobedience and the size of the school and the style of the school were not statistically meaningful. The returns on unsupervised playground incidents were small and therefore could prove to be very unreliable on chi-square testing. However, no statistically meaningful results were recorded.

Finally, the total results, excluding the category 'Others', were tested using chi-square and naturally the overall lack of relationship between the individual results and their parameters were reflected in the sub-totals. The somewhat surprising conclusion to be drawn from these results is that, with the exception of disobedience and type of catchment area, statistically there is no relationship between the most common types of disruption and either the social class the school serves, the size of the school, or the style of the school. Clearly the sample is small and only reflects the views of headteachers but there would appear to be a common perception of the most common types of disruption irrespective of the differing catchment areas served.

B. Most difficult types of disruption

The returns from headteachers on the most difficult types of disruption are tabulated in Table 4.5. With the exception of 'persistent irritant' the types of disruption in this category are completely different from 'the most common types of disruption. Generally headteachers placed into the 'persistent irritant' category those pupils who would interrupt their peers' work by snatching their property; by being physically or verbally abusive; or by general shouting out (at inappropriate times) in front of the whole class. Some irritants will make 'funny noises or animal noises and thus disrupt the concentration of all in earshot'. 'Persistent Irritants' proved to be the most difficult type of disruption for teachers to deal with because for some pupils this behaviour occurred frequently, and stopping them from doing it often proved to be very difficult and demanding of time. These findings parallel those of Wheldall and Merrett (1988) who suggested that it was the frequent, not the most heinous forms of pupil disruption that were most damaging to the quality and continuity of the pupils' learning.

Table 4.6 shows that headteachers in the survey considered that the most effective sanction against disruptive pupils was contact with their parents. This, the commonly held view, was also reflected in 'unsupportive parents' becoming the second most difficult type of disruption to deal with. It is evident from these two returns that headteachers should give parental contact a high priority.

The next two categories relate to times when the children are basically unsupervised. These include the myriads of incidents which can take place in the playground at break and lunchtime, and more specifically bullying.

Table 4.5: The most difficult types of disruption.

Type of dis-ruption	No. of returns		Returns subdivided by							
	Sc		Type of housing				Size		Style	
			1	2	3	S	M	L	O	C
1 Persistent	25 Ob	3	9	10	–		10	12	4	18
irritant	Ex	6.7	7.1	8.2	2.8		7.8	11.4	4.6	17.4
2 Unsupportive parents	20 Ob	4	2	6	–		6	6	3	9
	Ex	3.7	3.9	4.4	1.5		4.3	6.2	2.5	9.5
3 Playground sits (unsuper-vised)	17 Ob	3	2	7	1		6	5	3	9
	Ex	3.7	3.9	4.4	1.5		4.3	6.2	2.5	9.5
4 Bullying	16 Ob *	1	3	3	–		2	5	1	6
	Ex	2.1	2.3	2.6	0.9		2.5	3.6	1.5	5.5
5 Dumb insolence	10 Ob	1	2	3	1		1	4	0	6
	Ex	1.8	1.9	2.3	0.8		2.1	3.1	1.3	4.7
Sub-totals	Ob	12	18	29	2		25	32	11	48
	Ex	18	19.1	21.9	7.5		21	30.5	12.4	46.6
6 Others	9	Teacher/pupil clash, theft, uncontrolled tantrums, external family feuds								

Legend

Type of housing	Size of school	Style
1 – Mainly owner occupied	S – Small (<120 pupils)	O – Open plan
2 – Mixture of rented/owned property	M – Medium (120–220 pupils)	C – Cellular classes
3 – Mainly rented properties	L – Large (>220 pupils)	
SC – Score	Ob – Observed	Ex – Expected

Finally, dumb insolence, which means the child is prepared to offer little or nothing by way of verbal response to questions or requests but who by facial expression and/or by gesture indicate their non-co-operation/defiance of what is taking place at school.

None of the correlations between observed results and expected results show any statistical significance and therefore generally one must assume that the most difficult types of disruption for the primary headteachers consulted to deal with were common to all varieties of school, regardless of their social class, size or style. Overall the style appears to have least influence, with the observed results being reflected very closely by the expected frequencies. Similarly there is little difference between the observed and the expected results according to social class and likewise for the size of the school.

In conclusion, it must be assumed that the most difficult types of disruption are experienced in all varieties of schools regardless of social class, size or style. Secondly, it is suggested that the relatively minor but most frequent acts of disruption, as shown by a 'Persistent Irritant', is by far the most difficult situation to deal with long-term.

C. Most effective sanctions

The commonly held view is that parental contact is the most effective sanction. The returns from head teachers highlighted the evident fears of the pupils in having their parents involved at school. *It may be asked that if a pupil's fear relates to the parents, does the relationship between parents and children have equal importance as the regime of the school in determining pupils' predilection for disruption?* Is it the regime of the school or the role of the parents which has the greatest impact on pupil behaviour? Whatever the answer to the question the headteachers' view of the importance of the role of the parents in the discipline/behaviour of their children is quite clear. If parents have such a role in the discipline within schools, is this reflected in the opportunities for parental involvement and are they encouraged to do so? Perhaps this suggests the need, not only for consideration about the messages that schools send out to parents, but also co-operation with the parents in developing the schools' policies on discipline and the appropriate sanctions. These issues are discussed in more detail in Chapter 5.

The chi-square test (Table 4.6) revealed only one statistically significant result and that was between the style of the school and the sanction 'Positive Measures'. Schools described 'positive measures' as optimizing on opportunities to praise a pupil, for academic work or social behaviour, and by applying such praise present a very positive climate in which pupils would be much less inclined to be disruptive. Perhaps teachers in open plan schools would be more likely to take advantage of such approaches, but as the number of returns is small, too much credence should not be placed on this result.

None of the other results, either individually or collectively, were of statistical significance.

Parental contact was seen by schools as being very important in maintaining good behavioural standards and it might be argued that this type of sanction was second only to the suspension of privileges. The suspension of privileges as shown in the table was the second in the hierarchy of headteachers' preferred sanctions. However, together with loss of playtime, suspension of privileges would have the highest overall return.

The threat of being sent to the headteacher assumed a lesser importance than might have been expected, being just ahead of the use of a behaviour record which enables the school to keep a record of a pupil's behaviour, both good and bad, and through which daily parental contact is maintained.

Exclusion was seen as a relatively low order sanction and it can be argued that this is also reflected in the number of exclusions of primary aged pupils. The returns did not reflect different attitudes according to the three categories of school,

Table 4.6: The most effective sanctions.

| Sanction | No. of returns | | Returns subdivided by | | | | | | |
| | | | Type of housing | | | Size | | | Style | |
	Sc		1	2	3	S	M	L	O	C
1 Parental	35	Ob	11	13	11	3	9	23	10	25
contact		Ex	10.7	11.3	13	4.5	12.4	18.1	7.3	27.7
2 Suspend	28	Ob	8	8	12	2	9	17	7	21
privileges		Ex	8.6	9	10.4	3.6	9.9	14.5	5.9	22.1
3 Loss of	24	Ob	6	5	13	–	10	14	7	17
playtime		Ex	7.4	7.7	8.9	3.1	8.5	12.4	5	19
4 Removal	16	Ob	*							
to head										
teacher										
		Ex	4.9	5.2	5.9	2.1	5.7	8.3	3.4	12.6
5	14	Ob	3	4	7	1	4	9	3	11
Behaviour										
record		Ex	4.3	4.5	5.2	1.8	5	7.2	2.9	11.1
6 Lines/	13	Ob	5	4	4	1	5	7	5	8
Repetitive										
work		Ex	4	4.2	4.8	1.7	4.6	6.7	2.7	10.3
7 Exclusion	12	Ob	2	7	3	2	3	7	3	9
		Ex	3.7	3.9	4.5	1.5	4.3	6.2	2.5	9.5
8 Positive	5	Ob	2	1	2	–	2	3*	3	2
measures		Ex	1.5	1.6	1.9	0.6	1.8	2.6*	1.0	4
Sub-totals	147	Ob	39	50	58	13	48	86	40	107
		Ex	45.1	47.4	56.6	18.9	52.2	75.9	30.7	116.3

6 Others	8	Referral to Educational Psychologist/Detention Counselling

Legend

Type of housing	Size of school	Style
1 – Mainly owner occupied	S – Small (<120 pupils)	O – Open plan

2 – Mixture of rented/owned property

3 – Mainly rented properties

SC – Score

M – Medium (120–220 pupils)

L – Large (>220 pupils)

Ob – Observed

Ex – Expected

C – Cellular classes

* – x at 0.05 level of significance

nor did it reflect those schools which had already made use of exclusion procedure.

In conclusion, the schools' view on the most effective sanctions, statistically, do not relate to social class, the size of the school, or the style of the school.

D. Recommendations*

It could be argued that, as many of the recommendations from headteachers did not relate specifically to the socio-economic class, the size of the school or the style of the school, correlation by these three parameters would be pointless. However, initially for consistency, and secondly for the results that were extracted, the returns on recommendation were chi-square tested in exactly the same way as shown in Tables 4.4, 4.5 and 4.6 (Table 4.7). Overall, 36 relationships of these recommendations were chi-square tested against the three 'school' parameters. Three of these calculations showed a relationship that was statistically significant, the first one being the suggestion that access to psychological services be extended, with regard to the social class served by the school. Here, schools in socially deprived areas made more use of the psychological services, and would like to see them extended further.

The second significant result was that of the school having an exclusion room, to which disruptive pupils could be sent, relieving the class teacher of any immediate problems. This correlated with the type of catchment area of the school at a 0.05 level of significance. None of the schools serving the

Table 4.7: Recommendations.

Recommen-dation	No. of returns		Returns subdivided by							
		Sc	Type of housing				Size		Style	
			1	2	3	S	M	L	O	C
1 Improve	31	Ob	7	11	13	2	8	21	7	24
PTR		Ex	9.5	10	11.5	4	11	16	6.5	.24.5
2 Promoted	21	Ob	7	8	6	1	6	14	5	16
staff free		Ex	6.4	6.8	7.8	2.7	7.5	10.8	4.4	16.6
from class										
commitment										
3 Extension	19	Ob*	2	7	10	1	7	11	3	16
of Psycho-		Ex	5.8	6.1	7	2.5	6.7	9.8	4	15
logical										
Services										
4 Increase	10	Ob*	2	3	5	–	5	5	1	9
alternative		Ex	3.1	3.2	3.7	1.3	3.5	5.2	2.1	7.9
provision										
5 Exclusion	9	Ob*	–	4	5	–	2	7	1	8
room in		Ex	2.8	92.9	3.3	1.2	3.2	4.6	1.9	7.1
school										
6 Teacher	8	Ob	2	4	2	1	3	4	2	6
training		Ex	2.5	2.6	2.9	1	2.8	4.2	1.7	6.3
7 Educate	6	Ob	2	3	1	–	1	5	3	3
parents		Ex	1.8	1.9	2.3	0.8	2.1	3.1	1.3	4.7
8 Parental	6	Ob	1	2	3	–	1	5	1	5
liability		Ex	1.8	1.9	2.3	0.8	2.1	3.1	1.3	4.7
9	4	Ob	–	1	3*	–	4	–	–	4
Playground		Ex	1.2	1.3	1.5	*0.5	1.4	2.1	0.8	3.2
supervisor										
10 Simplify	3	Ob	–	1	2	–	–	3	1	2
exclusion		Ex	0.9	1	1.1	0.4	1.1	1.5	0.6	2.4
procedure										

Table 4.7: Contd

Recommen-dation	No. of returns	Returns subdivided by							
	Sc	Type of housing				Size		Style	
		1	2	3	S	M	L	O	C
11 Review school dis-cipline pol-icy	3 Ob	–	1	2	–	1	2	–	3
	Ex	0.9	1	1.1	0.44	1.1	1.5	0.6	2.4
Sub-totals	147 Ob	23	45	52	5	38	77	24	96
	Ex	36.7	38.7	44.5	15.6	42.5	61.9	25.2	94.8
6 Others	8	Configuration of school day, auxiliaries (classroom), more learning support staff, behaviour modification, playground equipment							

Legend

Type of housing	Size of school	Style
1 – Mainly owner occu-pied	S – Small (<120 pupils)	O – Open plan
2 – Mixture of rented/owned property	M – Medium (120–220 pupils)	C – Cellular classes
3 – Mainly rented prop-erties	L – Large (>220 pupils)	
SC – Score	Ob – Observed	* – x at 0.05 level of significance
	Ex – Expected	

better social areas made a return under this heading, contrast-ing with five schools in the poorer housing areas.

The third significant result was the relationship between playground supervision and the size of the school. The level of significance was at the 0.01 level, but as the size of the return was small, the importance of the results should not be over-emphasized. Playground incidents which occurred at times of non-supervision were to be found in the lists of both the most common types of disruption and the most difficult types of disruption to deal with. Given these facts, it is perhaps surprising that playground supervision did not have a higher profile in the list of recommendations. All the other results were assessed by chi-square test and proved to be of no significance statistically.

All the recommendations suggested, except the review of the school policy (low return), were based on changes in conditions outside the school and none related to the school adopting different approaches to the management of pupil behaviour. The majority of the returns related to a recommendation for improved staffing standards. However, few of these returns indicated how the additional staffing was to be used or how it was to help to resolve the problems created by disruptive pupils.

Parental contact was regarded by headteachers as the most effective sanction and was seen in similar light by pupils (see Chapter 3). Unsupportive parents was seen as one of the most difficult situations in which to have a positive impact on managing disruptive pupils. Despite these facts, the returns recommending improved school/home liaison were small. In summary, the main findings are as follows:

- With minor exceptions, the statistical analysis shows no relationship between the nature and solution of disruption, the type of catchment area, size or style of the school.
- Recognition is given to the importance of parental liaison.
- Pupils frequently causing minor disruption prove to be the most difficult for teachers to cope with.
- Increased staffing, in a variety of areas, is seen to be the most effective solution to disruption.
- The perceived need for change in school policy and practice is very low.
- Parental responsibilities are highlighted.

The teachers' perspective

The headteachers' perspective, while being very important, reflects their view of the state of discipline within the whole school and may be coloured by having to deal with the most difficult incidents of disruption and pupils who have a higher frequency rate for being involved in such incidents. Commonly it is the teachers who have to deal with disruptive incidents both in and out of the classroom. It is therefore appropriate that consideration be given to the teachers' view of discipline in schools and whether or not they share the media perception of ill-discipline in schools today.

The Scottish study examined the views of over 150 teachers about pupil behaviour in schools, through which a model of 'indices of misbehaviour' of pupils was developed. This research related to seven primary and 2 secondary schools (see Appendix E).

The results are summarized below :

- Pupil behaviour can vary considerably from year group to year group within the same school.
- Pupil behaviour can vary according to the regime of the school.
- 'Irritating' behaviour is more of a problem to teachers than 'diabolical' behaviour.
- Opinion about the deterioration of pupil behaviour through recent years varied markedly from area to area, with teachers in schools with 'poor' catchments generally agreeing that standards of behaviour had fallen.
- Boys are considered to be more disruptive than girls.
- Generally teachers consider that behavioural standards would improve with increased staffing, greater parental liaison/co-operation and schools reviewing their policies on discipline.

Some of the views of teachers represented here are reflected in other research. For example, all of the research programmes in recent years acknowledge the dominance of boys in disruptive behaviour; the work of Wheldall and Merrett (1988) mirrored the perception of teachers that the most disruptive behaviour to the effective delivery of lessons was the relatively minor but very frequent misdemeanours such as TOOT – talking out of turn; and that the quality of pupil behaviour can vary considerably from school to school (Rutter *et al.*, 1979; Lawrence *et al.*, 1984). However, other outcomes supported the most common anecdotal comments of teachers almost since the teaching profession began – such as 'class 2B' or 'the third year' are the worst group of children in the school. We are sure every teacher will have heard a similar comment myriads of times. While the sample is small the results most strongly suggest that the standards of behaviour from class to class and from year group to year group within the same school and at the same time can vary enormously. Clearly in terms of senior management this means that within the same regime and ethos of a single school the quality of the discipline and the standards of pupil behaviour can and do vary and in turn this must suggest that there are other parameters influencing the pupil's behaviour other than simply the school. This may be the pupil's home circumstances. It may be the self-esteem/self-concept of the pupil. The important fact is that there are parameters other than school which impact on pupil behaviour. Having identified that there can be substantial differences of pupil behaviour even in the same school regime, it is argued that it is then possible to identify when neighbouring primary schools were experiencing poor behaviour from the same cohort. Given this information, it is possible to forecast the secondary year groups which are potentially going to be particularly troublesome and this forecast provides an opportunity to make more appropriate resources available.

The ability to forecast future resourcing requirements will be considerably improved as the consequences of the 1993

Education Act and the Code of Practice have impact within the schools. Increasingly the staged response and the register of pupils with special educational needs will provide accurate data on those pupils with a tendency for disruptive behaviour. Such knowledge will help in identifying resource needs and priorities not only within the individual school but also, if data on primary schools is well co-ordinated, it will enable long-term planning in the secondary schools.

> ... all children with special educational needs should be identi-fied and assessed as early as possible and as quickly as is consistent with thoroughness ...
>
> (Code of Practice, 1994)

Concluding remarks

The evidence examined in this chapter creates a confusing picture about the importance, or otherwise, of schools in the standards of pupil behaviour. The climate created by Rutter *et al.* (1979) of the nature and regime of the school being the main determinant of the quality of pupil behaviour requires careful review. The longitudinal study of the exclusion record of the fifteen secondary schools and the closer scrutiny of the six schools for which there had been little change in the re-gime suggests that the closeness of the relationship between school regime and variations of perceived levels of disruption needs to be re-examined. The authors do recognize the impor-tance of the school, and particularly the quality of its man-agement, in creating an orderly and well-disciplined environment but would contend that it must be part of a shared responsibility. Pupils (see Chapter 3) see parents as having a very important role in their discipline. Similarly headteachers believe, *though they don't always show it*, that parents have an important role to play in the process of estab-lishing good behaviour. Both headteachers (and teachers) and parents have major impacts on the self-esteem and self-concept of the pupils. The nature of the pupils' feelings about themselves impacts on their response to 'authority', particularly in its form as a school.

How do parents perceive their role? Are they aware of how pupils feel about their involvement in discipline at school? Do they wish to become part of the policy-making process? The next chapter examines some of these issues and the prospects of parent/school partnership.

Bibliography

Abrams, F (1996) *Independent* newspaper (2 February 1996).

Blackham, G J (1967) *The Deviant Child in the Classroom.* Wodsworth Publishing Company.

Cohen, L and Cohen, A (1987) *Disruptive Behaviour.* Harper Education Series.

Cooper, P, Smith C J and Upton, G (1994) *Emotional and Behavioural Difficulties: Theory to Practice.* Routledge.

Coulby, D and Harper, T (1985) *Preventing Classroom Disruption: Policy, Practice and Evaluation in Urban Schools.* Croom Helm.

Crequer, N (1986) *Independent* newspaper (9 April 1988).

DES (1989) *Discipline in Schools: Report of the Committee of Enquiry chaired by Lord Elton.* HMSO.

DFE (1984) *Code of Practice on the Identification and Assessment of Special Educational Needs.* Central Office of Information.

DFEE Circulars (1994) *Pupils with Problems.*

Docking, J W (1980) *Control and Discipline in Schools.* Wheaton.

Galloway, D, Wilcox, B and Martin, R (1985) *Persistent Absence and Exclusion from School: The Predictive Powers of School and Community Variables.* British Educational Research Journal, 11.

Gilmore, C, Mattison, S, Pollack, G and Stewart, J (1985) *Identification of Aggressive Behaviour Tendencies in Junior Age Children.* Educational Review Vol. 37 No. 1.

Grunsell, R (1980) *Beyond Control: Schools and Suspensions.* Writers and Readers.

Hargreaves, D H (1984) *Improving Secondary Schools.* ILEA.

HMCI, Chief Inspector of Schools, OFSTED (1996) *Exclusions from Secondary Schools 1995/6.* The Stationery Office.

Lawrence, J, Steed, D, Young, P with Hilton, G (1981) *Dialogue on Disruptive Behaviour: A Study of a Secondary School.* PJP Press.

Lawrence, J, Steed, D and Young, P (1984) *Disruptive Children: Disruptive Schools.* Croom Helm.

Lowenstein, L F (1975) *Violent and Disruptive Behaviour in Schools.* NAS.

Lowndes, G A N (1969) *The Silent Social Revolution.* OUP.

McLean, A (1986) *An Analysis of Exclusions in Renfrew and Dunbarton.* SRC.

MacPhee, H (1987) *Exclusions: Disrupting Children in a Disrupting Situation.* SED.

Parsons, C (1995) *National Survey of LEAs' Policies and Procedures – for the identification of, and provision for, children who are out of school by reason of exclusion or otherwise.* Commissioned by the DFE and conducted by Canterbury Christ Church College.

Reid, K (1986) *Disaffection from School.* Methuen.

Reid, K (1987) *Combating School Absenteeism.* Hodder and Stoughton.

Rutter, M, Maughan, B, Mortimore, P and Ouston, J (1979) *Fifteen Thousand Hours: Secondary Schools and their Effects on Children.* Open Books.

Sanders D (1990) The Class Struggle. Unpublished PhD Thesis.

Skinner, A, Platts, M and Hill, B (1983) *Disaffection from School: Issues and Interagency Response.* National Youth Bureau.

Tattum, D P (1986) *Management of Disruptive Behaviour.* Wiley.

Topping, K J (1983) *Education Systems for Disruptive Adolescents.* Croom Helm.

Wheldall, K and Merrett, F (1988) It's Classroom Violence Time Again. *Teachers Weekly* 21 March 1988.

Wheldall, K and Merrett, F (1992) In Wheldall, K, *Discipline in Schools: Psychological Perspectives on the Elton Report.* Routledge.

Wragg, E (1988) *Wragg's Guide to Villains.* TES 28 October 1988.

5   Partnership with parents: a myth?

'The teacher says I must do it this way.' (every child at some stage)

Virtually every parent will have heard such a comment from their children at some stage. So who has the greatest influence on a child's education – teacher or parent? Is the need for a partnership between parents and school essential to fully developing children's potential? Is a real partnership achievable anyway? Do teachers feel threatened by the increasing demands made by parents? How are parents responding to the prospect of a partnership? Is partnership a myth?

Child development – a parental responsibility?

Conventional wisdom in the period up to the 1960s placed the burden of responsibility for the development of children on the parents.

> Another clear implication is that parents cannot reasonably expect to turn over much of the character training of their children to other people, whether in school, church or other youth organizations. By the very nature of character formation, no one other than parents can ordinarily have one tenth of their influence; and if the parents are continually reinforcing their own influence by their day-to-day treatment of the child, other adults can have little expectation of outweighing the parents' influence.
>
> (Peck, 1960)

In the 1960s the importance of the role of parents as almost the sole influence on the development of a child was rarely in question. The social infrastructure of the period implicitly supported such a view. Custodial sentences or residential placements were a common response to the anti-social behaviour of disaffected young people and this was based on the premise that the parents were inadequate or inept in responding to the challenging behaviour of their children. The 'Authorities' had to act to intervene and establish a more disciplined environment for the young people concerned and counteract the perceived poor quality of their upbringing. Inevitably this made manifest a potential conflict between parents and the 'Authorities'. The authorities could be any group in power but clearly included teachers, for they had most frequent and regular contact with children and could refer them to other agencies in authority such as the police and social workers and thereby exercise authority over the parents. This may lead to conflict between parents and the authority figure in this case teachers and headteachers. This emerged as the conventional wisdom of many educationists in the 1960s.

> Parents and teachers are natural enemies predestined each for the discomfiture of the other.
>
> (Waller, 1965)

Clearly this rather extreme view of the relationship between teachers and parents masks developmental work which was being undertaken during the 1960s. However, the teacher was the person in authority and most parents were passive participants in the education of their children.

Consideration of home/school liaison did not show any prominence until the late 1960s. Research in this area started in the early part of the decade (Musgrove, 1961; Wilson, 1962). Musgrove surveyed parents of primary-age children to seek comment on the role of the school and the parent (amongst other things) in dealing with children's behaviour.

The polarized views from this research were of either the schools or the parents bearing total responsibility for children's behaviour. However, in the middle of the continuum between the two extreme views, a response was developing to suggest that children's behaviour was an issue facing home and school together and consequently parents and teachers should develop closer relationships.

One of the first 'formal' signs of the value of a closer relationship between home and school was contained in the Plowden Report (1967). Plowden emphasizes the importance of good co-operation and liaison between parents and teachers. However, even at this time of 'enlightened' thinking, the emphasis was on the importance of parents being informed and indeed their views being sought on various issues, but it was made quite clear that it was the professionals who must be the decision makers and run the schools. The parental role was supportive rather than executive. Plowden was really an advocate of increased liaison with, but not increased responsibility of, the parents. The literature of the 1960s and early 1970s reflected this view of increased involvement of parents in education but their low participation in decision-making. The importance of authority and the subservient role of parents was evident.

Parents in the 1960s played, on the whole, a passive role but the new baseline for increased involvement and participation was laid. Gradually in the 1970s the position of parents in the life of schools developed. More information became available, in part through an increased awareness by teachers to provide more information and in part through statutory requirement. The voluntary expansion of the parents' involvement was mirrored in the work of Gibson (1980) in which through questionnaire and interview he reviewed the opinions of a number of parents about their involvement in the secondary school of 'Holbien'. On the whole the parents did feel they were involved in the school with over 90 per cent being satisfied with the quality and frequency of information provided through the 'newsletters'. Similarly the parents felt that the school provided a good source of contact through parents' evenings and through other opportunities to visit the school (94 per cent said they would not hesitate to make contact with the school if necessary).

Generally Gibson's survey indicated that parents felt they were well-served by the school in terms of information and general liaison. In spite of this only 39 per cent of the parents surveyed thought they had a good knowledge of the school. The outcome of this survey indicated that parents were happy with the quality of liaison between the school and home. Further, the survey indicated that parents did not wish to have a proactive role in the management and organization of the school – 88 per cent said 'no' to having more say in the running of the school. Parents saw the teachers as the professionals and in consequence any movement towards a parent/teacher partnership in which both parties have an equal role to play was not envisaged and by implication was not seen as desirable.

The approach of schools to parents generally changed during the late 1980s. The headteachers and teachers recognized the increasing importance of 'winning' a good parental perception of their school and how that impacted on the viability of the school through its ability to attract pupils. This new scenario emerged, initially quite slowly, following the 1988 Education Act. However, the momentum increased once its effects on school viability were realized and subsequently strongly supported by further legislation which enhanced the role and decision-making power of the parents.

> We have constantly emphasized the centrality of parental choice in our education reforms. It is built into the legislation governing the arrangements for grant-maintained status ... parents decide.
>
> (DFE News 95/94)

The practice in authorities regarding parental involvement and participation varies considerably but during the 1990s there have been several major projects initiated by authorities and designed to improve home/school liaison and to empower parents – e.g. Home–School Partnership In Oxfordshire 1992 and Us and the Kids, Development Education Centre (Birmingham) 1991. Such schemes gained the overwhelming support of teachers and headteachers:

> Effective communication between home and school is essential particularly in the present climate of rapid educational change.
> (Headteacher in Home–School Partnership In Oxfordshire 1992)

Relationships and influence today are centred around parents, politicians and schools. Parents, encouraged by political changes, are recognizing their opportunity to influence educational change. Equally their confidence is growing to take on the mantle of such responsibility and a desire to make their voice heard. In some respects this has become something of a symbiotic relationship with politicians who are using parental opinion of educational reform as an indicator of the perceived value of educational reform. Naturally the reciprocal of this is to use the opportunities of such reforms and resource allocation, such as the introduction of vouchers for nursery age children, to gain political acceptance. Schools, in their turn, are anxious to woo parents for good educational reasons but also as a part of being in the marketplace and therefore being determined to maintain viability by maintaining the school roll.

> So home–school relations are now firmly on the agenda of politicians, professionals and parents, albeit in different and changing ways. This is true literally as a consequence of cumulative legislation and formal opportunities for parents to be involved in the life and work of schools. It is also true metaphorically. Parents have become a strongly-felt, though often unseen, presence in the plans of politicians, in the daily work of education offices and in the work of schools. Above all, it has become necessary to accept that the creation and support of effective family-

school relationships is a necessary and legitimate concern, not an optional extra, as it was previously considered to be.

(Bastiani, 1989)

The past thirty years have seen significant changes in the accepted roles and responsibilities of parents of school-age pupils. Initially the parent was seen as the most important influence in their child's life in every respect, including the nature of the child's behaviour in school. The 1980s saw some change in this approach and even more dramatically in the 1990s. Simultaneously the conventional wisdom on the role of the school was being challenged.

Pupil behaviour – a school responsibility?

Rutter (1979) challenged the conventional wisdom of the 1970s which held parents almost totally responsible for the behaviour of children, and laid it firmly at the door of the schools. Rutter's influential text on the role of the school in developing appropriate behavioural responses from pupils concluded that schools were responsible for the quality of pupils *'behaviour, attendance, examination success and delinquency – even after taking into account differences in their intake'*. The pendulum was beginning to swing. Schools, not parents, were being perceived as the factor accounting for pupil behaviour, particularly among the disruptive children.

Almost overnight, the causal factor of pupil disruption being parents and home circumstances in the 1960s swung to being the nature and quality of the school in the 1980s. In both the 1960s and the 1980s there was an overwhelming desire on the part of researchers to identify a single or dominant causal factor of disruption in schools. Why is establishing a single causal factor of pupil such a holy grail? Do we need to have something or someone to blame? Why do we continue to attempt to solve complex problems with simple single solution answers? To swing from the view of near total responsibility of the parents for their children's behaviour to the near total responsibility of the school for pupil behaviour is reflective of the 'blame culture' in education. However, the range of parameters which may influence the development of children and young adults, while including parents and teachers, also includes peer pressure and sub-cultures, influence of other members of the family, changes in society, particularly levels of employment and changes in the work ethic, and influence of other youth organizations. The inherent character, personality, attributes and self-esteem of the individual will influence the way they think and therefore the ways in which they respond to all these various influences and equally have some bearing on their predilection, or otherwise, for disruptive behaviour. It is readily acknowledged that home and school circumstances will significantly influence pupil behaviour but these are two of a whole range of parameters influencing behavioural response.

> It is commonplace now that parental interest and encouragement affect a child's attainment and that they have important effects even when we have controlled our parental occupation and IQ. After all while a child may spend 15,000 hours in school (reference to Rutter (1979)), he will probably spend at least another 70,000 hours out of school and many of these will be spent with his family. We need to put as much effort into capturing the effects of these hours as we do into capturing the effects of those spent at school.
>
> (Heath and Clifford, 1980)

The extract taken from Heath's paper is part of a critical analysis of Rutter's work. Heath criticizes the methodology, data collection and statistical analysis of Rutter and suggests that many of Rutter's conclusions are flawed because insufficient account was taken of other parameters and the effect these would have on the results. One of these parameters was home background and the importance of parental influence. Much of the research, both before and after Rutter's conclusions were published, pointed to the relationship between home circumstances and success at school (Tizard, 1975; Pilling and Pringle, 1978; Docking, 1980; Reid, 1987). More recently the importance of parents' role in the education of their children has been recognized in the literature (Wheldall, 1992; Reynolds, 1992) and these changes in perception of the importance of the parental role have been reflected in increased parental rights provided through legislature.

Since 1980, education legislation has provided a steady increase in parental rights in such enactments as the following.

- **Education Act 1980** – the rights to express a school preference, receive information about the curriculum and organization of the school, and increased representation on governing bodies.
- **Education Act 1981** – the right to participate in assessment of special educational needs (SEN) and the annual reviews, a right to information and to appeal (in each case within limits).
- **Education (No. 2) Act 1986** – annual reports and meetings for parents, increased representation on governing bodies.
- **Education Reform Act 1988** – parental ballots on opting out, admission limits relaxed to allow open enrolment giving parents more chance to express preferences (of schools), the right to information on programme of work and progress.
- **Education (Schools) Act 1992** – the right to consultation before formal inspection (of schools), the right to reports on individual children, including examination and test results.
- **Education Act 1993** – independent tribunal to hear parents' appeals over children with SEN, Code of Practice for identification and assessment of SEN, rules governing school attendance and exclusion, tightened up, new rules for opting out ballots.

(Webb, 1994)

It is clear that the rights of parents and pupils have increased during the past decade in particular. However, parents do have ultimate responsibility for their children and at no time is this more evident to many parents than those first months and early years of their child's life.

Parents – the prime educators

Research on the influence of home and home circumstances on children's development, particularly in their formative years, placed great emphasis on the need for a caring, stable and consistent environment. These characteristics were seen as being essential prerequisites of successful child rearing (Coopersmith, 1967; Tizard and Rees, 1975). Studies of children who have not had this kind of upbringing suggest that children who are not so responsive to adult intervention have a tendency to physical and verbal abuse and are generally more difficult to control and to 'socialize' (Pilling and Pringle, 1978). Similar concerns underpin the Elton (1989) view of the important role of parents in the upbringing of their children, particularly during their formative years.

> We believe that socially responsible parenthood is particularly crucial in the first five years of a child's life. Parents must do everything they can to help children relate co-operatively to adults and to other children. They must also do their best to encourage their children to develop the attitudes and values on which both school and society are based. These include self-respect, respect and concern for others, self-discipline and moral qualities such as truthfulness and honesty. Some aspects of bringing up children may be instinctive. Others must be learned. Our impression is that, whereas many parents are highly skilled

in guiding their children towards adulthood, others are less so. A few seem not even to recognize the need for such skills at all.

(Elton, 1989)

The messages emerging during the 1980s were a confusing mixture of increasing parental responsibility for the sound development of educational provision based on a premise of parental expertise on the one hand, and an emphasis on highlighting the importance of parents developing adequate parenting skills, and the importance of them instilling socially acceptable characteristics in their children, on the other. In relation to the latter, research indicates the need for a stable environment for the children to thrive – but not necessarily the family home, providing that not being at home is not perceived as rejection. When both parents are going to work, it has been shown to be important that the parents, and the mother in particular, have some degree of job satisfaction so that employment is seen by all as positive (Docking, 1980).

The crux of the argument being put forward is that in a 'positive' situation children can feel good about themselves. They can have high self-esteem and self-concept, through which self-confidence will increase and difficult situations will be more easily tackled. Parents (or adults) need to provide a framework in which this can take place so that reasonable limits on behaviour are established, reflecting the absolute values of the parents, which if 'enforced in a non-punitive way are more likely to come to value themselves (the children) highly' (Docking, 1980).

Conversely in a negative situation the child will develop low self-esteem and the quality of behaviour and responses will be adversely affected. This can be intensified by changes in family circumstances – separation, divorce and broken homes leading to one-parent families. However, although the trauma of such histories can and does create behavioural responses from the children, it is difficult to correlate them directly. The single parent too readily sees what should be perceived as normal adolescent behaviour as attributable to the family circumstances (Ferri, 1975). A divorce or separation may bring to a close the scene of domestic strife and an end to the stress and strains, which in turn may be of benefit to the child (Davie, 1978). Later research suggests that children require a stable, consistent situation in which there is a clear direction of behavioural expectation, delivered in a supportive, non-threatening and non-punitive way, and which is commonly understood by both parents and teachers (Docking, 1980; Sanders, 1990).

Research undertaken in the 1980s emphasizes the importance of the parental role in creating the right environment for their child and the significant influence that they had in shaping their development. The research (Tizard and Hughes, 1984; Watt and Flett, 1985) suggests a role for the parents and mothers in particular, as the 'Prime Educators'. The theme, similar to that of Heath and Clifford (1980), is that children spend the majority of their time in the family setting and are affected by the role that adults adopt, particularly the parents and particularly mothers, in the child's pre-school years. Understandably, the quality of the input by the parents will relate in part to their own self-perception.

> The key factor ... seems to be the power and prestige which mothers feel in their role.
>
> (Watt and Flett, 1985)

In the situation where the mother has high self-perception and feels valued in her role, the better the environment she will create for her child. The needs of the child will be assessed more accurately and provision and stimulation will be provided more appropriately to meet these needs (McCail, 1981). The perceptions of the mother will relate to her own circumstances and how she is regarded within the family. Earlier research suggests that this related quite closely to the social status of the family.

> ... middle-class parents do not treat success as a prize reserved for the intellectually brilliant but act on the assumption that it lies within the grasp of any industrious child of their own ... working class parents ... accept signs of failure as evidence that a child lacks the required ability .... Parental attitudes have been identified as a persistent source of working class underachievement.
>
> (Roberts (1980) in Craft *et al.* (1980))

Polarizing the response of people into two categories is an over-generalization, a point that Roberts made, and the nature of the categories is also debatable. However, the sentiments of the two extremes and the continuum between them is a more acceptable view of parental perception. If the nature of parental perception impinges on the child and the child's development, it follows that the upbringing of the child will vary from the very positive to the very negative. These attitudes may reflect upon the child, be mirrored by the child, and thereby influence the child's behaviour. However, the way in which the child will respond will be dependent on their own character, attributes and self-esteem.

Pupil behaviour: a joint responsibility of parents and teachers?

> Parents are a major determinant of children's behaviour. It is important for the school to establish a good and early working relationship with the parent of a child who may have emotional and behavioural difficulties. If the child does not respond readily to the concerted efforts of home and school, then wherever possible both will need to draw on the established partnership in their efforts to find a solution.
>
> (DFE Circular 9/94)

The importance of a good relationship between home and school for pupils with a tendency towards EBD (emotional and behavioural difficulty) is evident. Equally so it is with all parents. Relationships have to be established over a period of time and require an input from both 'partners'. Parental attitudes may influence responses of children to their school and affect the reciprocal response of teachers. Reid (1987) argues that the school must keep the parents fully informed so they can play a full part in both the negative and positive aspects of their child's development and thereby increase responsibility and accountability. He suggests that regular face-to-face contact of teachers with all parents would enhance the parental role and demonstrate the importance that the school places on parental involvement. Other research added weight to Reid's argument that enhancing the parents' self-image would improve the prospect for the child (Raven, 1980; McCail, 1981). Reid (1987) cited the system in France of pupils acquiring 'confidence, skill levels and socialization'. He suggested these personal developments accounted for the low level of disruption recorded, which in turn was directly attributable to the high level of responsibility placed on the parents, the quality of provision and the co-operation among teachers, parents and the community, which permeates the whole system.

Therefore the importance of parental attitudes and the parts the community and the school have to play in forging those attitudes must be stressed, so children gain a more positive and ambitious home background which will help to develop their confidence and social skills and in turn may reduce pupil propensity for disruption.

Consequently the movement towards increased parental/school liaison is essential and its value is generally well accepted:

> ... one thing is clear ... that very general acceptance exists of the desirability of forcing links between home and school, of clearing away barriers to communications and sources of misun-

derstanding between teachers and parents about the education of their children

(Taylor in Craft *et al.* (1980))

This statement of intent of Taylor has become the reality central to many parent-partnership schemes which have developed around the country:

According to this view (partners in education including parents), the professional expertise, autonomy and status of the teacher is unchallenged, but it is recognized that a highly significant aspect of teachers' professional expertise and commitment should be collaborating effectively with children's parents to optimize the educational provision that the school can make. Some of the starting points in thinking through this position are the following:

(i) all parents are educators and very influential ones; other educators, like schoolteachers, can be most effective by planning their contributions in relation to the central contribution of parents;

(ii) unless teachers can persuade parents to value what they are offering their children at school, they will be unlikely to persuade the children to value it;

(From Home–School Partnership In Oxfordshire 1992)

At the present time the argument for improved liaison is well established, but it is debatable whether or not this will develop into a truly equal partnership of parents and teachers. If the general principle of good parental/school liaison is accepted, the need for such links becomes even more acute in the case of disruptive children – 'parents are a major determinant of children's (who may have EBD) behaviour' (DFE 9/94).

Pupil behaviour – views of parents and teachers

Given the conventional wisdom in the 1960s to 1970s and in the 1980s of the dominant factor affecting the behaviour of children being home circumstances and school circumstances respectively, Sanders (1990) developed a research programme to consider the perceptions of parents and teachers. The main theme was pupil behaviour but in this area of the research the focus was taken from a parental perspective. How had schools informed parents about the nature and ethos of the school, particularly those areas related to discipline and sanctions? Did parents feel that their child's school had kept them fully informed of school activities and their child's development?

Three elements of the research programme informed the debate about the importance and quality of the relationship between parents and teachers. First, as part of a questionnaire on pupil behaviour and discipline in schools, headteachers made comment on the importance of parental co-operation in resolving poor behavioural patterns of difficult pupils. Secondly, the school prospectuses of 67 primary and fifteen secondary schools from one urban area were reviewed. Thirdly, cohorts of parents from two secondary schools and their feeder primary schools were surveyed by questionnaire; a small group were interviewed.

Parents and discipline: the headteachers' view

Headteachers consider parents to have a significant role in the behaviour of pupils at school (see Chapter 3). The view was expressed that in cases of pupils who were disruptive, unsupportive parents considerably exacerbated the problem. The lack of support could be made manifest by either refusing to liaise with the school staff at any level or by not being prepared to co-operate with the school. Therefore the pupils could be placed in a position where they lack clear direction and controls because of the dichotomy between parents and teachers. The headteachers placed great importance on such co-operation from parents and establishing a common approach to effectively deal with disruptive pupils.

As a part of such co-operation both parties need to be aware of, mutually approve of, and actively support any measures which are introduced. These could be programmes designed to modify behaviour or sanctions given as punishment against the pupil appropriate to the level and type of disruption. In consideration of the most effective sanctions, the importance of parental contact was highlighted both by headteachers (Chapter 4) and pupils (Chapter 3). Headteachers emphasized the importance of parental support in dealing with disruptive pupils. Pupils regarded parental involvement with the headteacher as an effective sanction.

Given these facts it would be reasonable to assume headteachers would make every effort to welcome parents into the life of the school, to establish good relationships from the outset and to develop a mutual understanding and appreciation of the ethos of the school. If such a baseline can evolve during 'normal' circumstances then the likelihood of parent/teacher co-operation in more difficult circumstances – dealing with a child's behavioural problem is enhanced. Clearly this places great emphasis on the importance of home/school liaison. Such liaison can be developed through information circulated by the school and by providing opportunities for face-to-face contact.

Headteachers' recommendations (Chapter 4) on means of improving responses to the management of disruptive pupils included parental contact and co-operation. However, it appeared very low down the list of priorities and in a way which can only be described as condescending – increasing parental liability and suggesting that parents need further education on how to exercise care and control of their children. It was evident therefore that on the one hand schools viewed parental contact in dealing with disruptive pupils as very important and yet, on the other, parents should know their place in the school organization.

Parents' initial contact with school – the prospectus

For many parents the first contact with the school will be via the school prospectus. The prospectus assumes an important role in opening the dialogue between parents and teachers. Is it user friendly? Was it written with parents in mind? Did parents of children at the school have any part in preparing or reviewing it?

The school prospectus is a statutory requirement in which the inclusion of certain information is a legal obligation. Essentially it is designed to be informative but also helpful and supportive to parents. The Scottish study included consideration of intention of two aspects of the school prospectus. First, does it provide the parents with a suitable introduction to the school; secondly, and more specifically in terms of disruptive pupils, what approach is taken in the prospectus to explain the discipline policy to parents?

Prospectuses from 67 primary and fifteen secondary schools were analysed on the following themes:

- presentation (layout, use of jargon, personal letter of intro-duction from the head teacher etc.)
- strategies for home/school liaison (newsletters, parents' evenings, access to school, PTA etc.)
- discipline policy (rules and regulations, and codes of con-duct).

The quality of presentation varied enormously. Nearly half the schools had used a high quality cover, but for many this made the contrast of a very poorly presented content even more stark. This aspect was much less common among the prospectuses of secondary schools than those of primary schools. Further, since the time of the research it must be acknowledged that the quality of school brochures in every sense has improved enormously and there are no longer the same marked differences between the quality of primary and secondary school prospectuses. Nevertheless at the time of the research the differences between the quality of school brochures from the two phases were evident – only six of the primary prospectuses had drawings or photographs whereas in the secondary prospectuses these were commonplace. Clearly the means of producing prospectuses and the expertise available were far more sophisticated in the secondary than in the primary schools but the desire of the headteachers to market their schools via the brochure was evident.

Many of the schools (44 per cent) made use of a letter of introduction, of which three headteachers had signed the prospectus personally, and a further thirteen had a letter bearing the head's signature. The latter touch, Edgar (1988) argued, helped to personalize the prospectus, and thereby increase its effectiveness as an aid to good home/school liaison.

Strategies for home/school liaison were generally well presented. Almost 80 per cent of schools made direct reference to the importance of contact between home and school; 66 per cent mentioned the use of newsletters or information leaflets as a means of keeping parents up to date with school activities; and 60 per cent outlined the use of parents' evenings to provide information on children's academic and social development. Schools commonly (60 per cent) referred to the existence of Parent/Teacher Associations (or other similar support groups) through which the parents could become more closely involved with school activities and general support of the school. However, the governing body of the school was only referred to in 40 per cent of the prospectuses. Thus a statutory body on which parents should be represented was only referred to in a minority of cases. Discussion with several headteachers suggested this was an oversight rather than an attempt to exclude the parents, but may reflect badly on the level at which parental involvement is aimed by most schools. As with the issue of the quality of prospectuses, the more recent editions have corrected these shortcomings but the authors would suggest that such omissions are reflective of some headteachers' view of the importance of parental involvement. Similarly a minority of prospectuses made some comment about parents as school helpers and did so at a variety of levels. These varied from the relatively mundane preparation of rough books and flash cards to the more ambitious support to teachers in reading programmes, design and technology and computing.

Occasionally the prospectus emphasized the school's role as an authority, stressing the importance of parental responsibility and accountability. It was evident that schools which included these comments wished to improve understanding of the parenting role. However, it is likely that the impact on parents may undermine the school's initiative on improving teacher/parent liaison because the tenor of the specific comments was: 'badly judged and potentially damaging to relationships'.

The prospectuses showed considerable variation in the coverage of the discipline and sanctions policy. None of the prospectuses made reference to the parental involvement in the preparation of the school's policy on discipline and sanctions, though again in discussion with headteachers, it was evident that in some cases parents had been fully involved in either the early planning stage of the policy or in a review of a draft policy. Additionally, those schools which were in a process of reviewing their discipline policy were doing so with at least a modicum of parental involvement.

Almost half the schools (46 per cent) had placed the section on pupil discipline in the last quarter of the prospectus and of these, the majority were literally at the end of the booklet. A small minority (7 per cent) had elected to draw up a statement on discipline which was completely separate from the booklet, but which was given out to parents along with the school handbook. Of the schools which placed their policy at the end of the booklet some 67 per cent discussed the school ethos, including the development of pupils' self-esteem and developing esteem for their position in the school and society generally, before mentioning any rules and regulations associated with this aim. The schools which were anxious not to over-emphasize the rules and regulations attached to their school society also attempted to encourage positive attitudes to develop co-operative behaviour rather than simply lay down the rules and regulations and attached sanctions.

A small minority (4 per cent) placed the 'rules and regulations' section at the beginning, giving the impression, often erroneously, of a school preoccupied with discipline and sanctions. The remaining schools had given a lesser prominence to the discipline policy in the body of the prospectus.

The level of detail covered in the 'behavioural' section of the prospectus varied enormously. The highest number of rules identified in a handbook was 38 and, in contrast, others simply referred to a code of conduct. As might be anticipated, the school with 38 rules placed them on the first page of the prospectus and left no doubt as to what the school stood for!

It might be expected that the natural progression from the statement of the rules and regulations applying to a school would be associated sanctions. Surprisingly, over a third of the school prospectuses made no reference to sanctions whatsoever. In the remaining cases the sanctions followed sequentially the section on the rules and regulations, or formed an integral part of that section. Six schools admitted to only one sanction (school referral to parents) and 75 per cent of the schools had five or fewer sanctions laid down. These included a range of approaches such as written exercises (though generally not lines), withdrawal of privileges, reporting to the headteacher, parental contact, regular behavioural reports and exclusion. Although many of these sanctions were simply punitive, some were designed to aid behaviour modification, e.g. the daily report system.

None of the prospectuses made any reference whatsoever to the sanctions and discipline policy being produced in conjunction with the parents. However, in a small minority of cases, parents had been involved in the preparation or review of the policy. Such an approach would help to emphasize the value of the parental/school partnership. Further, schools which make no mention of the sanctions used to enforce its discipline policy cannot expect its parents to fully co-operate in their application. Consequently, in such circumstances it would be virtually impossible for them to work with the school in sustaining and extending the school's general philosophy.

In conclusion, it appeared that the quality of the school handbooks was highly variable, many of which would benefit from a review of the content, presentation and tenor relating to parental perception. This applied particularly to the sections on the school's 'code of behaviour and sanctions' which must be more sensitive to the parental reader and more explicit, if full parental co-operation and understanding of the school's aims are to be achieved. Indeed, after the findings of the research programme were published, many of the schools did revise the prospectus.

Do the schools meet parental expectations?

In order to assess the success of schools in forging links with the home, parents were surveyed by questionnaire covering five main areas: (a) the schools propensity for welcoming parents into the school, (b) the quality of information about the school, (c) their rights to send their child to the school of their choice, (d) the discipline policy and their desire to be involved in developing the school's discipline policy, (e) any other areas of parental interest/ concern.

Two contrasting areas of relatively low (Vernall) and high (Macgill) socio-economic status were selected and, in each, four cohorts of pupils' parents were surveyed. These included first year primary and secondary pupils, final year primary pupils and 14-year-old pupils who had already embarked on option courses for presentation at 16+. These groups were selected because parents of first year pupils would have experienced the school's induction programme; parents of final year primary pupils should have theoretically the most extensive knowledge of primary home/school liaison and, at the time of the survey, would have had an opportunity to visit their local secondary school in readiness for their children's imminent transfer; and the parents of the oldest cohort surveyed would have been consulted about subject choices.

The responses from the parents of primary pupils were as follows:

- 401 (73 per cent) responses were received from a potential of 550
- at first year primary stage Vernall returned 64 per cent and Macgill 78 per cent
- at final year primary stage Vernall returned 67 per cent and Macgill 78 per cent

The responses from the parents of secondary pupils were as follows:

- 323 (69 per cent) responses were received from a potential of 474
- at first year secondary stage Vernall returned 54 per cent and Macgill 88 per cent
- at third year secondary stage Vernall returned 44 per cent and Macgill 64 per cent

Do parents feel welcome?

Generally (over 90 per cent) parents of primary pupils felt welcome in their child's school even when popping in to the school without an appointment. The returns demonstrated a parental perception of there being adequate opportunity to visit the school and that they were kept fully informed about their child's development both socially and academically. There was no significant difference in the perception of parents from the two contrasting areas.

Parents of the secondary pupils from the Macgill area had a similar view of the welcome and opportunities as their primary counterparts, 98 per cent felt that the approach made by the school was very positive. The vast majority (72 per cent) of the Vernall parents agreed with this response but a significant minority found the secondary school much more imposing and therefore difficult to feel 'at home'.

However, parents did suggest that the opportunities to visit and the welcome provided by the school could be enhanced by:

• giving longer notice and greater details of school activities
• arranging more informal events to meet the teachers
• providing creche facilities.

Quality of information about the school

Returns from the parents suggested that the vast majority of parents were very happy about information made available by the school. Most had found the handbook useful and easy to understand, although the majority would have found it helpful to have had the handbook updated more frequently.

Newsletters, school magazines and general letters home kept parents, on the whole, well informed of school activities. Few of the parents thought there was a need for much more information about the school. It was evident that parents greatly appreciated the efforts of the school to provide information. It was also clear that parents appreciated the quality and quantity of information which was provided for them.

The section of the study which analysed school handbooks did not attempt to review them on a school by school basis, but it is worthy of note that the handbooks represented 'scored' fairly highly in that analysis. Some parents commented on ways in which information could be improved as follows:

- more information on extra-curricular activities
- more information on subject choices
- more frequent newsletters
- more organizational information – class sizes, resources, timetabling etc.
- more on examinations and grading
- generally more information on the curriculum.

Rights of parents to choose schools

It is now reasonable to assume that the right of parents to select the school of their choice is well known to parents. Of the parents of first year primary pupils 94 per cent were aware of this facility, 98 per cent of parents of upper primary pupils, 99 per cent of parents of first year secondary pupils and 98 per cent of parents of third year secondary pupils. Obviously with these extremely high levels of returns, there was no significant difference between the returns of the Macgill area and those of the Vernall area.

Overall, the level of parents who had opted to use this facility was small, with 86 per cent of first year primary pupils attending their local zoned school, 88 per cent of upper primary pupils, 74 per cent of first year secondary pupils and 80 per cent of third year secondary pupils. However, the point was made by several of the parents interviewed that the selection of the local zoned school was one of choice and their way of exercising their rights under the Parents' Charter.

Discipline in school

Comments on the school's discipline and sanction policy reflected the greatest dichotomy in parental thinking. Approximately three-quarters of the parents of first year primary pupils were aware of their school's discipline policy but only half were aware of their school's sanction policy. In this area of the questionnaire there was little difference in the returns from the two areas. By upper primary the level of parental knowledge of the school's discipline policy had increased to approaching 90 per cent and almost three-quarters were aware of their school's sanction policy. Again there was little difference between the returns of the two geographical areas. At secondary level parental knowledge of both the discipline and the sanction policy was much higher, with the lowest return being on sanctions at some 85 per cent and the highest on discipline at 94 per cent. The majority of parents who stated that they were unaware of the school's discipline policy felt they should have a detailed knowledge of the school's approach to behavioural management.

Response to parental involvement in developing the school's discipline policy varied enormously. At first year primary level there was close compatibility between the two areas with some 61–75 per cent of parents in favour. Parents of upper primary pupils seemed to be slightly less keen to be involved with a range of 56–70 per cent for the Macgill primary schools and 52–94 per cent for the Vernall primary schools. At secondary level the overall responses were lower still with 50 per cent of parents of first year pupils at Macgill and similarly 60 per cent for the Vernall area. With the parents of pupils in the third year the figures were 62 per cent for Macgill and 74 per cent for Vernall.

The figures suggested that the majority of parents, and on occasions a significant majority, would wish to be involved in developing the school's discipline policy. Some parents commented that their involvement should be liaison and consultation over appropriate sanctions and others that parents should be elected to a policy-making group and thereby enable parents to make a more significant contribution to the school's procedures.

Other comments from parents

A small minority of parents suggested additional areas for the school's consideration. These were as follows:

- Discipline should be strengthened.
- Corporal punishment should be re-established.
- Parents are too subjective and should not be actively involved in the discipline of children.
- Uniform should be compulsory.
- Parents should have the right to see their child's file at any time.
- More information should be made available on the curriculum and teaching methods.
- Any changes of policy should be by consultation with the parents.

Even at a cursory glance it is evident that the subjects of discipline and curricular change figured very highly. The concerns about discipline were felt in both areas although there was a prevalence for concern about the curriculum in the Macgill area and much more interest shown in discipline in the Vernall catchment. The expectation of parents was that the quality and frequency of information would develop, and indeed there was a genuine desire to have more contact with the teachers. However, there was no suggestion of a change of approach or balance within the relationship between teachers and parents. The unwritten message of the vast majority of returns showed that parents were happy to be the passive partners of the relationship and that schools were expected to be the active and proactive members of the relationship.

In summary the responses from parents revealed a parental perception that:

- they had adequate opportunity to visit the school;
- information received from the schools was viewed as being of high quality and circulated frequently;
- they had a sound knowledge of the school's discipline policy;
- they were aware of their rights under the Parents' Charter;
- there was much more dubiety about the role of parents in developing and maintaining school discipline policies;
- there was a general expectation /aspiration for the school to be the proactive partner in any home/school liaison.

Conclusion

The development of an equal partnership between parents and the school seems as far away as ever – perhaps it is an unachievable, possibly even an undesirable goal. What is clear is that in terms of discipline and behavioural policies within schools, for different reasons pupils and headteachers have strong views on the role and importance of parents in that process and procedure. Pupils with a propensity for disruptive behaviour will be better supported by earlier intervention by schools which includes harnessing the experience and expertise of parents in a partnership approach.

> Schools on their own do not make a lot of difference; but the ways in which schools relate their efforts to their students' home lives, and enable parents to relate their own educational efforts to their children's school lives, make massive differences.
>
> (McIntyre, 1992)

Bibliography

Bastiani, J (1989) *Working with Parents: A Whole School Approach.* NFER Routledge.

Coopersmith, S (1967) *Antecedents of Self-esteem.* Freeman.

Craft, M, Raynor, J and Cohen, L (1980) *Linking Home and School.* Harper and Row.

Davie, R (1978) *Social Developments in the Education of the Young Child.* Open Books.

Docking, J W (1980) *Control and Discipline in Schools.* Wheaton.

DES (1989) *Discipline in Schools Report of the Committee of Enquiry chaired by Lord Elton.* HMSO.

DFE Circulars(1984) *Pupils with Problems.*

DFE News 95/94.

Edgar, J (1988) Unpublished MEd Thesis.

Ferri, E (1975) *Background to Children in One Parent Families.* Therapeutic Education Vol. 3.

Gibson, R (1980) *Teacher/Parent Communication.* CIE.

Heath, A and Clifford, P (1980) *The Seventy Thousand Hours that Rutter Left Out.* Oxford Review of Education Vol. 6 No. 2.

McCail, G (1981) *Mother Start.* SCRE.

Musgrove, F (1961) *Parents' Expectations of the Junior School.* Sociological Review.

Oxford Home–School Partnership In Oxfordshire (1992).

Peck, R F and Havinghurst, R J (1960) *The Psychology of Character Development.* Wiley.

Pilling, D and Pringle, M K (1978) *Controversial Issues in Child Development.* PE.

Plowden Report (1967) *A Report of the Central Advisory Council for Education, Children and their Primary Schools.* HMSO.

Raven, R (1980) *Parents Teachers and Children.* Hodder and Stoughton.

Reid, K (1987) *Combating School Absenteeism.* Hodder and Stoughton.

Reynolds, D (1992) *School Effectiveness: Research, Policy and Practice.* Cassell.

Rutter, M, Maughan, B, Mortimore, P and Ouston, J (1979) *Fifteen Thousand Hours: Secondary Schools and their Effects on Children.* Open Books.

Sanders, D (1990) *The Class Struggle.* Unpublished PhD Thesis.

Tizard, B and Hughes, M (1984) *Young Children Learning.* Fontana.

Tizard, B and Rees, J (1975) The Effect of Early Institutional Rearing on Behaviour Problems and Affective Relationships of Four-Year-Old Children. *Journal of Psychology and Psychiatry*, 8, 16.

Waller, W (1965) *Sociology of Teaching.* Wiley.

Watt, J and Flett, M (1985) *Continuity in Early Education.* AUP.

Webb, S (1994) *Troubled and Vulnerable Children: A Practical Guide for Heads.* Croner.

Wheldall, K and Merrett, F (1992) in Wheldall, K, *Discipline in Schools: Psychological Perspectives on the Elton Report.* Routledge.

Wilson, B R (1962) *The Teacher's Role: A Sociological Analysis.* British Journal of Sociology (13).

6 Exclusions and the law: policy makes perfect?

Introduction

> In recent years concern has been widely expressed by, among others, headteachers, professional associations, local education authority (LEA) officers, teachers and politicians about behaviour and discipline in schools. That concern has been particularly but not exclusively focused on the rise of the number of pupils permanently excluded from school.
>
> (Chief Inspector of Schools, 1996)

The mid-1990s has seen unprecedented change in the policies of Local Education Authorities in England on the identification and provision for disaffected pupils. The demand for change was encapsulated in the 1993 Education Act and supported by a series of guidance papers from the then DFE (Department for Education, now Department for Education and Employment). These guidance papers were designed to support change in special education generally but included a set of six papers aimed at 'Pupils with Problems', e.g. 'The Education of Children with Emotional and Behavioural Difficulties' and 'Exclusions from School'. The papers published in May 1994 in essence obliged local education authorities to review their existing policies and for many necessitated substantial change. The drive for change, it is argued, was influenced by several parameters – public opinion on discipline in schools and its impact on the political process, an increasing acceptance from educationists that special education should be about including pupils and not excluding them and in this respect the adverse effect of league tables on schools' practice on the admission and exclusion of pupils.

Concern about the quality of discipline in schools had been increasing during the 1980s and 1990s and was often reflected in the media.

> Verbal and physical attacks by pupils on teachers are increasing and the attackers are getting younger ...
>
> (Ngaio Crequer, *Independent*, 9 April 1988)

> Nine out of ten teachers say that discipline is deteriorating, according to a survey published yesterday ... There were 293 assaults on teachers in the past year in 28 areas where detailed records were kept. Staff were worried about their safety from pupils, parents and intruders ...
>
> (Fran Abrams, *Independent*, 2 April 1996)

Such statements typify the journalistic view of what was, and perhaps what is, happening to discipline in schools today. Keith Morris of the NAS/UWT reported in 1988 that indiscipline in schools was increasing and that children as young as 5 and 6 were becoming disruptive. Morris went on to say that teachers had been given black eyes, had been kicked, bitten, had their hair pulled and had been attacked with knives and had had their cars vandalized. Similar opinions have been expressed in the media over the past ten or fifteen years. The alleged collapse of behavioural standards in schools was, and is, so frequently stated that insidiously it is becoming the conventional wisdom that schools are battlefields of pupils against teachers.

Often, and understandably, the response from the media is highly subjective but it may be reflective of public opinion or indeed lead it. The danger is that as only the sensational appears to make the news it overly directs the conventional wisdom. Nevertheless the degree of public disquiet with standards of behaviour in schools has been recognized. The

157

Government response to such mounting adverse public opinion in the 1980s was to establish a Committee of Inquiry into Discipline in Schools, more commonly known as the Elton Report (1989).

> The Committee of Enquiry into Discipline in Schools was established by the Secretary of State for Education and Science in March 1988 in response to concern about the problems facing the teaching profession. Our task was to recommend action to the Government, local authorities, voluntary bodies, governors, headteachers, teachers and parents aimed at securing the orderly atmosphere necessary in schools for effective teaching and learning to take place.
>
> (Elton Report, 1989)

The Elton Committee set out to achieve these laudable aims and within the Report there are summary sections intended to support teachers, schools, pupils, governors, local education authorities and even the Government. However, the level of advice and indication of the way forward in each of these areas was relatively limited, e.g. there were thirteen main recommendations for teachers, summarized in the following statement:

> We conclude that the central problem of disruption could be significantly reduced by helping teachers to become more effective classroom managers. We see the roles of initial and in-service training as crucial to this process. This leads us to make two key recommendations. The first is that all initial teacher training courses should include specific practical training in ways of motivating and managing groups of pupils, and of dealing with those who challenge authority. The second is that similar in-service training should be provided through school-based groups. These groups should aim not only to refine classroom management skills, but also to develop patterns of mutual support among colleagues.

Our evidence suggests that the status of teachers has declined in recent years, that this decline was accelerated by their recent protracted industrial action, and that it may have reduced their authority in the eyes of pupils and parents. We recommend that all interested parties should give urgent consideration to establishing a framework of relationships between teachers and their employers which will minimize the risk of future industrial action. We also ask the Secretaries of State to clarify the legal basis of teachers' authority.

We emphasize the serious implications that any teacher shortages would have for standards of behaviour in schools, and the need for their pay and conditions of service to be such as to ensure the recruitment retention and motivation of sufficient teachers of the required quality.

(Elton Report, 1989)

While the Elton Report created interest at the time of publication it did little to take schools further forward or influence operational practice. Nevertheless it did support the view of contemporary research, that the popular emerging opinion of schools being in a state of anarchy with physical abuse being commonplace, is an inappropriate reflection of schooling as a whole based on a small but unrepresentative sample of sensational cases of pupil disruption.

Press comments have tended to concentrate on attacks by pupils on teachers. Our evidence indicates that attacks are rare in schools in England and Wales. We also find that teachers do not see attacks as their major problem. Few teachers in our survey reported physical aggression towards themselves. Most of these did not rate it as the most difficult behaviour with which they had to deal. Teachers in our survey were most concerned about the cumulative effects of disruption to their lessons caused by relatively trivial but persistent misbehaviour.

(Elton Report, 1989)

The main contribution of the Elton Report was to highlight and collate issues of concern to parents and pupils in a less emotive way than the more sensational headlines in the press. It also provided an influential government-commissioned document which provided the impetus and baseline from which several other innovations were initiated. One such programme was the Bullying Research Project which was funded by the DFE between 1991 and 1993 and undertaken by the University of Sheffield directed by Prof. P. Smith. This work culminated in 1994 with the publication by the DFE of *Bullying: Don't suffer in silence* – a pack designed to combat bullying in schools. The pack has been well received in many schools and provides both a good background to the issue of bullying and sound practical advice on how to tackle it in schools. It also provides some indication of the levels of bullying taking place in schools today.

Table 6.1: The extent of bullying. (Source: *Bullying: Don't suffer in silence* (DFE, 1994))

Primary schools	At least sometimes (%)	At least once a week(%)
Being bullied	27	10
Bullied others	12	4

Secondary schools	At least sometimes (%)	At least once a week(%)
Being bullied	10	4
Bullied others	6	1

The statistical database of pupils with behavioural problems was also extended by the introduction of a national scheme to record permanent exclusions. This was undertaken as an initiative by the DFE as a 'National Exclusions Reporting System' which reported 2910 permanent exclusions in 1990/91 compared with 3833 in 1991/2. Research commissioned by the DFE and reported by Canterbury Christ Church College in 1995 suggested a known level of permanent exclusion of 10,624 (returns from 101 of the then 109 LEAs) and an estimate of 11,181 exclusions for the whole of England (see Chapter 4). A similar exercise completed for 1995/6 (which following the emergence of several new unitary authorities was based on 91 usable returns from 117 English authorities) revealed a known level of permanent exclusions of 10,999 and an estimated total for England of 13,581 (Parsons, 1996). The reasons for these apparent rapid increases in the rate of exclusion can only be interpolated as yet but there is speculation that the expanding number of excluded pupils is the result of schools' sensitivity to their performance in the league tables and a consequent desire to remove pupils whose performance adversely reflects the school either academically or more commonly behaviourally.

The imposition by government of crude performance indicators, such as rates of public examination success and truancy, may well lead some schools to abandon pupils who are likely to bring performance scores down. Individual teachers, too, might be increasingly inclined to seek the removal of disruptive pupils from their classes, rather than attempting to deal with the problem behaviour in the classroom. This would be an understandable response if teachers were to feel that their own performance, and possibly their job security, were to depend, in part at least, on the quality of pupil behaviour observed in their classrooms by appraisers. On the other hand, the provisions of the Children Act (1989) make it a duty of schools and teachers to take careful account of pupils' welfare needs and, where necessary, pass information to Social Services Departments. This places teachers in a key position, with regard to pupils' welfare needs. In light of these circumstances, there has never been a worse time than the present to be a pupil experiencing emotional and behavioural difficulties in school or a more challenging time to be a teacher faced with 'difficult' pupils.

(Cooper *et al.*, 1994)

Schools' income is dependent on their ability to attract pupils and thereby maintain or increase their roll. Clearly such an ability to sustain their school roll relates to their reputation within the community. Naturally the quality of the reputation will depend to a large extent upon the perception of the local community of the school's standards particularly in terms of pupil behaviour and academic achievement.

Earlier research (SED, 1980) suggested that the key factor for parents to select a secondary school for their children was academic achievement. While the academic reputation continues to be of importance, growing parental concern about behavioural standards can significantly influence secondary school selection (Sanders, 1990; KMBC, 1995). For many parents one significant characteristic of a school's willingness to 'deal' with difficult pupils is the exclusion record of the school. For many parents there has to be a balance between too high an exclusion rate suggesting poor discipline and too low a rate which can create a perception of schools being lax in their approach to discipline. In financial terms the apparent anomaly between schools wanting to attract resources and yet being financially penalized as a result of excluding pupils can be resolved by viewing the two processes at different levels – exclusion leads to losses at a micro level but may attract an increased admission which would then impact on the school budget on a more macro scale, both in terms of numbers and over a more extensive timescale. If the increase in the number of exclusions is any reflection of these processes with a threefold increase in permanent exclusions during the past three years, it would appear that macro considerations outweigh the micro factors. The steady rise in the number of pupils being permanently excluded and the associated public concern was one element which led to further legislation and guidance on the exclusion of pupils.

Education Act 1993 impact on exclusions and pupils with SEN

The 1993 Education Act in conjunction with the Code of Practice has had a major impact on the wider aspects of the identification, assessment and provision for pupils' with special educational needs. These apply to all aspects of special educational needs, including pupils with emotional and behavioural difficulties. The Code of Practice was effective from September 1994 and provides guidance to LEAs and schools in particular and a variety of other agencies such as support services, social and health services. The main themes are to provide early identification of pupils with special educational needs and the nature of provision to meet those needs. It also provides advice and a recognized procedure to involve appropriate agencies at each of the five stages recommended in the guidance. The process of assessment in the school (stages 1 to 3) and possible subsequent statutory assessment (stage 4) may lead to the completion of stage 5 of the Code of Practice, i.e. the issue of a Statement of Special Educational Needs. Pupils identified and provided for through this process generally will have an individual education programme (IEP). For most pupils this will mean that their special needs will be recognized, and provided for at an earlier stage. The process also requires early involvement of parents which together with a tailored IEP may help some pupils who have behavioural problems to respond positively and avoid the serious sanction of exclusion.

The 1993 Education Act and DFE Circular numbers 8/94, 10/94 and 11/94 outline changes in the law on exclusion and offer guidance on procedures and perceived good practice. These introduced numerous procedural changes designed to ensure some standardization across the country and to prescribe the timescale in which parents, schools and LEAs should operate.

Circular number 8/94 provides guidance on 'Pupil Behaviour and Discipline'. The guidance is aimed specifically at schools and governing bodies and suggests the development of whole-school policies on behaviour. The Circular highlights the main roles of the teacher, the headteacher and the governing body. In respect of teachers good practice is deemed as creating 'a calm and purposeful classroom atmosphere' in which careful task matching to the pupil's ability has been undertaken and the characteristics below are evident:

- procedures are clearly understood regarding pupil discussion, participation in lessons, movement in class, the way in which work is handed in, and what pupils should do when tasks are completed;
- explanations are clear;
- work requirements of pupils are clearly set out, and progress is monitored carefully; clear instructions are given so that activities run smoothly. Misbehaviour is handled quickly and calmly so that the pace of the lesson is not lost and further disruption is minimized;
- teachers develop good listening skills, and react appropriately to pupils' responses;
- work set is appropriate to pupils' abilities;
- clear goals are set for each work activity and all pupils understand them before an activity begins;
- lessons start and end on time;
- classrooms are suited to activities as far as possible;
- seating arrangements are suitable. These will often be dictated by the activity but particular attention should be paid to the location of the more troublesome pupils and those easily distracted;
- external interruptions are minimized whenever possible; and
- necessary materials for a given activity are available.

(DFE Circular 8/94)

The guidance recognizes that even with good preparation and delivery of a lesson there may be occasions when disruptive behaviour takes place. In such situations it exhorts teachers to have a range of strategies available to quickly restore order. One such strategy may be to seek support from senior staff including the headteacher. The headteachers' role within the Circular is given most prominence and this also reflects the views of the importance of the role and responsibility vested in the senior management team, particularly the headteacher, as perceived by the Elton Committee (1989). The seven elements of a headteacher's responsibility in maintaining good discipline in their school as perceived by the Elton Committee are reiterated within the guidance, i.e.

- staff management;
- establishing and maintaining internal and external communication systems;
- fostering a sense of community;
- taking the lead role in setting aims and standards;
- encouraging collective responsibility;
- supporting staff; and
- directing overall curriculum and organizational planning.

(Elton Report, 1989 and DFE circular 8/94)

The role of the headteacher and staff in maintaining high behavioural standards is featured in much recent research and guidance (Gillborn *et al.*, 1993; Cooper *et al.*, 1994; Chief Inspector of Schools, 1996). As part of that role particular emphasis should be placed on relationships with parents.

Policy and practice on working with parents

I find with the teachers, if you have got a problem and you phone up, there is always someone to see you. You can bring your child along and try and sort it out. There is a kind of spirit in the school where you feel welcome. When you go to some schools to see the headteacher, you have got to 'sit here' and 'wait', you know.

(Parent in Gillborn *et al.*, 1993)

The way in which relationships develop between parents and the school is important for all pupils but most particularly so for pupils with behavioural problems. Often when the relationships between staff of the school and parents are good, pupils presenting problem behaviour can have their needs identified and met in a unified response from both home and school which often proves to be the most efficient and effective way of moderating misbehaviour. Where such relations have not developed and parents remain hostile to the school and school staff appear to take little cognisance of the parental perspective, the pupil is much less likely to receive a clear message of what is required and the problem behaviour remains unresolved.

The majority of individual teachers who wrote to us suggested that the attitudes and behaviour of some parents were major causes of bad behaviour by their children in school. We were told that the factors involved ranged from family instability, conflict and poverty to parental indifference or hostility to the school ...

We believe that parents have a vital role to play in promoting good behaviour in schools. There is much that they can do on their own initiative, but they also need the help and encouragement from schools. We felt that two research findings were particularly interesting in this connection. About 900 secondary pupils in the West Midlands were asked in a survey which reward for good work or behaviour in school they valued most, and which punishment for bad behaviour they feared most (Wheldall and Merrett 1988). A positive letter home was one of two rewards most valued. The punishments most feared were also those involving parents – a letter home or being put 'on report'.

(Elton Report, 1989)

The findings of Wheldall and Merrett (1988), echoed in the Elton Report, relating to the importance of the parental role and therefore the priority which schools should place on developing good relationships with parents, was strongly reflected in the work of Sanders (1990) and in the HMI Report *Parents and Schools* (1991). Many schools have adopted an active role in welcoming parents into the life of the school, establishing a parents' room, organizing adult courses and extending this approach to the whole community. Commonly this approach gives a higher focus of the school within its community which gives significant benefits to the school – not least of which will be better surveillance of the school building. However, such a user-friendly approach will pay dividends in providing for most pupils with behavioural problems – particularly the younger pupils, who have at primary phase and early secondary proved to be most responsive to such intervention.

The changing practice to increasingly involve parents is well-steeped in the policy changes of the 1990s. The Education Act 1993 and the Code of Practice place great emphasis on very early contact, liaison and involvement of parents with pupils with special educational needs including those pupils with emotional and behavioural difficulties. Similarly the regulations and guidance on exclusions demand good communication and liaison between the school and the parents much before an exclusion is to be contemplated. This approach should lead to many pupils with emotional and behavioural difficulties being identified earlier, parents becoming involved earlier and the chances of a resolution of the behavioural problem in the pupil's mainstream school being much improved. Inevitably this will not apply in all cases and may lead to the headteacher having to consider excluding the pupil. The DFE Circular 10/94 does provide appropriate guidance.

Prerequisites to exclusion

The main thrust of the new guidelines (DFE 10/94) was to prevent injudicious and inappropriate use of exclusions. Guidance is given on the type of pupil background or case history which may lead to headteachers considering exclusion as a course of action.

Preliminary Factors to Consider

Any punishment should be appropriate to the offence, and each incident of poor behaviour needs to be examined individually in the context of the establishment of the established school behaviour policies with which staff, parents and pupils are familiar, and, if appropriate, in the light of the criminal law. However, the fact that a form of behaviour could constitute a violation of the criminal law should not, in itself, be taken as automatically leading to exclusion or as relieving the school of the responsibility to give the matter individual and separate consideration. Exclusion should be used in accordance with the principles set out below. In determining the need and duration of any exclusion, the head teacher should in all cases first consider the following factors in relation to the behaviour:

- the age and state of health of the pupil;
- the pupil's previous record at that school;
- any particular circumstances unique to the pupil which might sensibly be taken into account in connection with the behaviour, e.g. strained or dramatic domestic situations;
- the extent to which parental, peer or other pressure may have contributed to the behaviour;

- the degree of severity of the behaviour, the frequency of its occurrence and the likelihood of it recurring;
- whether or not the behaviour impaired or will impair the normal functioning of the pupil or other pupils in the school;
- whether or not the behaviour occurred on school premises or when the pupil was otherwise in the charge of the school staff, or when the pupil was on the way to or from school. An important consideration in cases of doubt is the extent to which behaviour away from school had a serious impact on the life of the school;
- the degree to which the behaviour was a violation of one or more of the rules contained in the school's policy on behaviour, and the relative importance of the rule(s);
- whether the incident was perpetrated by the pupil on his or her own or as part of a group (using one pupil as a scapegoat should always be avoided); and
- whether consideration has been given to seeking the support of other agencies, such as the education welfare service or educational psychology service.

(Paragraph 21, DFE Circular 10/94)

The Circular 10/94 provides the most definitive advice on exclusions at national level ever to be made available. Nevertheless it is recognized that, while superficially desirable, it is not possible to be entirely prescriptive about excluding a pupil. What are the circumstances in which it is appropriate to exclude a pupil? How bad does the misbehaviour have to be before a pupil's misbehaviour warrants an exclusion? The various 'DFE' circulars recognize the important role of headteachers in exercising their judgement to balance the various factors which lead to terminating a pupil's right to be admitted to a school. The dilemma of making such decisions is reflective of the difficulties in changing the terminology describing a pupil from 'normal' to 'disruptive' (see Chapter 4). The vast majority of exclusions are fixed-term periods which by definition lead to the pupil returning to their 'own' school. Pupils who are excluded permanently will have their existing school place terminated and the nature, range and quality of educational provision which may follow is extremely diverse. The 1993 Education Act made provision for these two types of exclusion only.

The demise of the indefinite exclusion

It is in relation to exclusions that the 1993 Education Act had one of its greatest impacts. The main change relates to the reduction in the types of exclusion with schools now not being able to set 'indefinite' periods of exclusion from school.

> Under the Education (No. 2) Act 1986 (the 1986 Act), exclusions from LEA maintained schools could be fixed period, indefinite or permanent. A similar provision exists in the articles of government of self-governing (grant-maintained (GM) schools. Section 261 of the Education Act 1993 (the 1993 Act) abolished the category of indefinite exclusion. This change in the law has effect on both LEA and self-governing (GM) schools regardless of any contrary provisions which may exist in the school's articles of government. The 1993 Act also sets a limit for fixed period exclusions of up to 15 school days in any one term. The purpose of these changes is to prevent exclusions lasting longer than is warranted, and to remove the uncertainty involved in indefinite exclusions.
>
> (Paragraph 8, DFE Circular 10/94)

These new measures were introduced in September 1994 and therefore it is too early to assess their long-term effectiveness but the demise of indefinite exclusions may result in an increase in the number of permanent exclusions and therefore create an outcome contrary to that anticipated. Regardless, this change, as far as all excluded pupils are concerned, will be an improvement on previous practice because 'final' decisions will have to be taken and some form of alternative education made available. No longer do schools have the option to exclude indefinitely and therefore pupils are now either re-admitted after an exclusion or permanently excluded. They are not left in the unsatisfactory limbo of the indefinite exclusion.

Experience suggests that schools had one of two approaches to indefinite exclusions. The first was the very responsible and responsive approach to the pupil's needs where the indefinite exclusion was used as a means to make a different provision from the school resources and facilitate monitoring until more appropriate educational provision could be made. The second approach of schools to indefinite exclusions may have been perceived as quasi-permanent exclusions. In such cases it is less likely that there would have been any form of tutoring or monitoring of the pupil or referral to another agency. Such lack of support often led to further deterioration of the pupil both academically and socially.

Permanent exclusions

The rules and regulations relating to exclusions are made clear in the 1993 Education Act and the supporting guidance in Circular 10/94 from DFE It is anticipated that all preventive measures have been exhausted and that permanent exclusion is being used as a last resort. The new guidance explains the timescale in which procedures have to be completed and provides more explicit guidance on the parental means of appeal against the headteacher's decision to exclude. Generally the new guidance makes the whole operation of exclusions much tighter and less open to individual interpretation. As stated earlier one of the most significant changes in the 1993 Education Act is outlawing of indefinite exclusion.

This will remove the potential for headteachers to use the indefinite exclusion as a quasi-permanent exclusion. The positive and negative aspects of this change have been referred to already but it should also be noted that home–school agreements/trial admissions no longer have any legal status. Home-school agreements have frequently been used as a vehicle acceptable to the school and the pupil/parent to permit the pupil's re-admission to school. While this is still a possible informal cause of action it no longer has any legal status.

> Home-school agreements which specify conditions to be met which have been agreed between the school, the pupil and the parent, can be useful in setting out for parents their particular responsibilities in relation to their child and in defining the school's role and policies. But they have no legal basis. They are voluntarily entered into after the child has been awarded a place, and should not be included in the school's admission criteria. The breaking of such an agreement is not in itself sufficient reason to exclude a pupil either for a fixed period or permanently. Instead the headteacher should consider whether the particular offence itself warrants exclusion, regardless of the agreement's existence.
>
> Similarly, schools may not admit pupils on a trial basis, give pupils a lower priority in admission arrangements or refuse a pupil admission on the grounds that he or she may disrupt the education of other pupils. If, once admitted, the pupil is found to be seriously disruptive, then proper procedures must be followed as for any other pupil. This is particularly important if, in due course, a further exclusion were to be considered necessary
> ...
>
> (DFE Circular 10/94)

The reduced status of home–school agreements or 'conditional re-admissions' seems to be in neither the pupil's nor the school's interests. Schools may be more inclined to move to a permanent exclusion because they cannot enter a contract with the pupil and/or parent which has any recognized status. This is likely to lead to some pupils being permanently excluded who previously would have been given another opportunity of returning to school. Ironically the research on the use of 'conditional' exclusions in the area which made most use of them, Scotland, suggests that approximately 50 per cent of pupils who were conditionally returned to school following exclusion successfully reintegrated into their original school and without further exclusion (Sanders, 1990).

Similarly headteachers when admitting pupils need to ensure that any new pupil's presence in the school is not going to be seriously detrimental to the physical or educational well-being of other pupils and yet the new guidelines seem to suggest otherwise. This direction in the guidance also runs contrary to the approach adopted to pupil placement in the Code of Practice for pupils at stage 5. Such confusion in the guidance is not helpful to the school but equally, obliging pupils to consider mainstream schools at a time when they have demonstrated that they are failing in a similar situation seems irrational. If the view is that the original school should not have permanently excluded the pupil, surely in line with the rest of the Code of Practice the issue should have been tackled at source.

Provision for permanently excluded pupils

The 1993 Education Act and supporting Circular 11/94 from the DFE places a new duty upon local education authorities.

Section 298 of the Education Act 1993 requires that LEAs:

> should make arrangements, for children of compulsory school age, for the provision of suitable full-time or part-time education at school or otherwise than at school if by

reason of illness, exclusion from school or otherwise, they may not for any period receive suitable education unless such arrangements are made for them; and

may make similar arrangements at their discretion for children above compulsory school age but less than 18.

(DFE Circular 11/94)

The range of educational provision made to pupils who have been permanently excluded from school is quite wide. The largest percentage (38 per cent), according to recent figures, will have their education provided through a Pupil Referral Unit (PRU). The next largest group of approximately 30 per cent will receive 'home' tuition. Other (16 per cent) pupils when permanently excluded from one mainstream school may be almost immediately admitted in another mainstream school. This is particularly common in the primary phase. The nature of provision for the remaining pupils includes Further Education, the independent sector and voluntary agencies. (Figures taken from a survey Commissioned by the DFE and conducted by Canterbury Christ Church College, 1995.)

Re-integration into mainstream schools

It is difficult to obtain accurate figures of the number of permanently excluded pupils who return to mainstream. Even more difficult is establishing how many return directly to another mainstream school without any other form of intervention or assessment of the pupil's needs. The most recent research suggest figures of between 27 per cent of primary-age pupils and 15 per cent of secondary pupils (Survey by Canterbury Christ Church College, 1995) return directly to mainstream schools following an exclusion. While this is thought to be an underestimate it indicates that only a small minority of pupils who have been permanently excluded are returned to mainstream schools. This is hardly surprising when headteachers are advised to use permanent exclusion very sparingly for pupils with extreme behavioural records and consequently such pupils are unlikely to be welcomed into another mainstream school. The threefold increase of permanently excluded pupils since 1991/2 may present a different picture but this may relate more to the accuracy of the database than a significant change in the approach of headteachers to managing pupils with behavioural problems.

It should also be noted that many authorities do provide a system of supporting and assessing excluded pupils other than in mainstream schools. Generally these are designed to establish the precise nature of the pupil's needs prior to identifying appropriate provision. In this respect the exclusion is used to highlight the level of the pupil's needs and to recognize that at that stage mainstream school is not the most appropriate educational option. Consequently to immediately admit the excluded pupil into another mainstream school would not always be in his/her interest as without assessment or support he/she may yet again be predetermined to fail. This applies most particularly to the older pupils – years 10 and 11.

Pupil Referral Units (PRU) and tuition

Provision made for excluded pupils has commonly been in special units which provide individual tuition and/or class teaching in small groups. The nature of such provision has varied considerably from authority to authority and the Education Act 1993 has addressed this issue by naming all such provision as Pupil Referral Units and in Circular 11/94 providing more specific guidance on their operational framework.

PRUs are schools, but the nature of existing off-site units makes it impracticable for them to be subject in full to the same legislative requirements as mainstream schools. They are typically small, have limited staffing, resources and accommodation, cover a wide age range and have a rapidly changing roll. Schedule 18 to the 1993 Act, and the regulations made under that Schedule, therefore make a number of adaptations in respect of PRUs to the law applying to schools. The key differences relate to the curriculum to be offered in PRUs, premises requirements, dual registration of pupils in PRUs and schools, and the relative duties of LEAs and teachers in charge of units.

(Circular number 11/94 DFE)

The more detailed regulations give advice on the management of PRUs which does not include a requirement to have a governing body, relaxes considerably in comparison with mainstream schools the requirement to provide the National Curriculum and makes allowance for part-time placement of pupils. However, it is anticipated that pupil placements will be short-term prior to return to other provision, mainly envisaged as mainstream schools, and that consultation on the organization and procedures of the PRU will take place with 'feeder' schools. Similarly the guidance on PRUs places emphasis on the multi-agency needs of pupils so provided and encourages the close involvement of social service departments, the police and other agencies (Knight, 1995).

PRUs commonly provide a service which is broader than making small class provision for excluded pupils. For example, some have and continue to be used to provide education for pregnant schoolgirls and nursing mothers of school age. The guidance suggests that for many of these pupils mainstream school is a more appropriate location. However, the main and often integral service which PRUs will provide is individual tuition. This may be used in a preventive way to assist pupils to maintain mainstream places. Alternatively they may provide assessment and support services to meet the needs of excluded pupils and help to develop them in preparation for alternative educational placement in potentially a range of other types of educational establishments. These may include small classes in the PRU, mainstream primary or secondary schools, special schools both MLD and EBD, Colleges of Further Education, independent and voluntary educational services.

The latest analysis of pupils who have been excluded and subsequently provided for at a PRU suggests that:

> One quarter of the primary pupils for whom there are records attend PRUs while nearly 40 per cent receive home tuition. The corresponding proportions for secondary pupils are 39 per cent in PRUs and 27 per cent receiving home tuition.
> (Survey conducted by Canterbury Christ Church College for DFE, 1995)

The emerging role of Colleges of Further Education

The number of statutory age school pupils who attend Colleges of Further Education, while very small, is significant. The colleges provide an important additional resource in the range of educational provision to meet the needs of pupils who have been permanently excluded from school. Colleges of Further Education are referred to specifically in the DFE Circular 11/94.

> In line with the Department's grant letter to the Further Education Funding Council, colleges in the FE sector were advised by the FEFC that in 1994/5 the Council expects colleges to enrol students of compulsory school age in exceptional circumstances only ...
> Nevertheless, it may be appropriate for some Year 10 or 11 pupils who are out of school to go into further education, including a sixth form college ...

But in particular cases the education available in a college may meet an individual pupil's needs, bearing in mind his or her age, ability and aptitude and any special educational needs that he or she may have. In such circumstances placement in a college may offer a suitable and effective way of providing education in accordance with section 298 of the 1993 Act.

(DFE Circular number 11/94)

The statistical information available currently on the number of pupils so provided for in FE colleges is incomplete but figures based on the autumn term 1994 indicate that approximately eight per cent of the excluded pupils have their educational needs met in FE colleges. Anecdotally, many pupils known to the authors and who, following exclusion and individual support, have been enrolled at their local college have had improved patterns of attendance. Some have also achieved creditable performances in the GCSE examinations.

Other provision for excluded pupils

The range of all other types of provision account together for just in excess of 10 per cent of permanently excluded pupils. These included some of the charitable trust initiatives in the voluntary sector such as Cities In Schools which provide a mixture of facilities for disaffected pupils but of which perhaps the best known are the bridge courses for Year 10 and 11 pupils. These projects demand and generally achieve high levels of attendance from pupils on each of the three main elements which include time at the local FE college, work experience and supervision, and counselling. It also includes the collaborative schemes of which the most common is the local authority based education and social services combined departmental projects. These collaborative schemes together accommodate nearly 50 per cent of pupils provided in the 'other' category. The remainder include both private sector and voluntary services initiatives.

Concluding position statement

The 1993 Act, and its accompanying guidance papers, did not impact on local education authorities and schools until September 1994, and at the time of writing, while approximately half of the authorities have produced new policies, many are still reviewing provision or consulting on new proposals on exclusions and provision for excluded pupils. Consequently it is suggested that within this area of education there will continue to be a rapidly changing picture. It is likely that the trend of the increasing number of pupils being excluded will continue as the competition in mainstream schools to 'capture' new pupils and maintain their rolls (and their income) bites even deeper.

Bibliography

Abrams, F (1996) *Independent* newspaper (2 February 1996).

Chief Inspector of Schools, OFSTED (1996) *Exclusions from Secondary Schools 1995/6*. The Stationery Office.

Cooper, P, Smith C J and Upton, G (1994) *Emotional and Behavioural Difficulties: Theory to Practice*. Routledge.

Crequer, N (1988) *Independent* newspaper (9 April 1988).

DES (1989) *Discipline in Schools: Report of the Committee of Enquiry chaired by Lord Elton*. HMSO.

DFE (1994) *Bullying: Don't suffer in silence*. HMSO.

DFE (1994) *Code of Practice on the Identification and Assessment of Special Educational Needs*. Central Office of Information.

Gillborn, D, Nixon, J and Ruddock, J (1993) *Dimensions of Discipline: Rethinking Practice in Secondary Schools.* DFE/HMSO.

HMI (1991) *Parents and Schools: Aspects of Parental Involvement in Primary and Secondary Schools.* DFE.

HMI (1991) *Parents and Schools.* HMSO.

KMBC (1995) *Choosing a School: The views of parents, pupils, teachers and local authority staff.* Marketing and Corporate Research Division, Knowsley Metropolitan Borough Council.

Knight, R (1995) *Educational Provision for Excluded Pupils.* NFER/EMIE.

Parsons, C (1996) Survey of Permanent Exclusions in England 1995/6. Letter to Chief Education Officers, 28 November 1996.

Parsons, C (1996) Permanent Exclusions from Schools in England: Trends, Causes and Responses, in *Children and Society*, 10.

Sanders, D (1990) The Class Struggle. Unpublished PhD Thesis.

SED (1980) *SED: Talking About Schools: Survey of Parents' Views in Schools Education in Scotland.* HMSO.

Wheldall, K. and Merrett, F. (1988) It's Classroom Violence Time Again. *Teacher's Weekly*, 21 March 1988.

7 Youth, disaffection and society: some concluding thoughts

Introduction: youth and society

The transition to adulthood for young people is complicated by the fact that there are few symbolic 'rites of passage' in modern society. The adolescent's route towards adulthood is not marked out by clearly defined signposts. For example, at 16 years of age an adolescent can marry or join a trade union yet cannot be tattooed or own a house or flat; and at 17 years the adolescent can drive most vehicles, buy a firearm, hold a pilot's licence, join the military, yet cannot vote, serve on a jury or make a will! Hence, in addition to the fairly dramatic physical changes of puberty which herald the teenage years, each adolescent must try to establish a sense of personal significance and self-esteem, look for a personal philosophy and set of values, aim for independence and adjust towards it. New relationships with adults and authority figures need to be negotiated and roles clarified in respect of peers, and with the opposite sex.

Further, over the past fifteen years or so we have seen the development of consumerism and the establishment of the primacy of the market-place, together with its influence on the occupational and social landscape of young people's development. This has occurred at a time in Britain when the behaviour of adolescents has come under increasing scrutiny by policy-makers and when, despite an overt focus of specific sorts of young people's rights being protected in law, there has been an erosion of autonomy and a depletion of individual rights particularly those related to independence which is one of the hallmarks young people seek in approaching adulthood (Jones and Wallace, 1992). Manifestations of our rapidly changing society appear in various guises: satellite television, international information networks (the Internet) and personal computers create possibilities for globalization in terms of communication and information which, in turn, influence individual values, desires, choices and taste. Supported by the growth of multinational companies, consumerism and the ascent of service industries enable individuals to access the global market-place to create lifestyles which express their particular customs, fashions, roles, social choice and tastes (especially if they have the financial resources to access the consumer market widely). Further, it is possible for people to portray a range of 'styles' since there can be a variety of overlapping groups with which they can identify and within which they can play roles associated with everyday social networks.

In connection with this Maffesoli (1996) suggests that social life is now conducted through a variety of relatively transient, fluid and fragmented – though often regular – social groupings, such as workplace colleagues, hobbyists, interest groups, sports club members, sports fans, interest groups, environmental movements and consumer lobbies. These heterogeneous 'fragments', which he claims are the remainders of mass consumption, are groups distinguished by their shared lifestyles and tastes: these he calls 'post-modern neo-tribes'. (Such groups have the power to integrate and include, to create solidarity, but are less 'influential' in excluding.) Hence changing Western societies contain within them a multiplicity of overlapping social groups, distinguished by shared values, dress, adornments, rituals, stages of membership and with particular roles to enact as sources of group identity. However, it must be stressed that these are temporary identities which render social status somewhat ambiguous. Such an interpretation offers the proposition that 'tribal' values are replacing the ethical orientations of Durkheim's (1964) 'conscience collective' and traditional morals. Additionally, it highlights the possibility that certain 'tribes' can create and exploit countervailing forces, such as ethnic nationalism or xenophobic fascism, within modern societies.

With regard to adolescence, Maffesoli's writing suggests that the more permanent and 'visible' youth sub-cultures of the 1970s and 1980s described by Brake (1985) and others have given way to other forms of social collectivity. For young people supporting soccer teams, discos, pubs, night clubs, youth organizations of various types, raves and so on may represent the social networks of these youthful tribes. Yet for some young people involvement in these tribal networks may, at once, be more problematic in terms of opportunities and availability of cash to 'tune in' to these lifestyles, and by the influence of what Matza and Sykes (1961) in a different context call the 'subterranean' values of social class.

Social shifts have created new constraints, experiences and opportunities for adolescents, in a context where even well-established social institutions can be subject to change. The family unit is one example of how a social institution has developed a variety of models in recent times. The nuclear family is now juxtaposed with 'reconstituted' families, shared custody arrangements and single-parent homes. Additionally, changes in social attitudes and expectations have occurred in many spheres of life. To cite two examples: access to illicit drugs is now a common feature of growing up for many young people; and the transition from school to full-time employment has become highly problematic. Thus there are many social challenges to young people in modern Britain.

Within the chapters of this book we have attempted to outline the complexities and multifaceted nature of disaffection, and by exploring the interrelationships among social factors, the school context and the individual's developing self image – in part from the young person's perspective – we have offered pointers towards future policy implementations which may enable young people to engage meaningfully with adult society.

Young people and families

Within the post-war period higher divorce rates and changes in family living patterns have produced many more single parent units and 'reconstituted' families. Nevertheless, it is difficult – and misleading – to correlate behavioural problems or social disadvantage with particular family types or with a breakdown of the traditional nuclear family group. Of as much significance may be parenting styles.

Parenting styles may be important to the ways in which young people develop social roles. Hendry *et al.* (1993) found crude social class differences in parenting styles, but a finer grain analysis revealed considerable variety across social classes and of particular interest is the clear identification of a family style associated with multiple problems for the young person. While an authoritative parenting style tended to be associated with middle-class families and a permissive style tended to be linked to working-class families, there were, however, a substantial number of permissive middle-class families (Hendry *et al.,* 1993). Two other styles were identified across the social classes – authoritarian and neglectful. The neglectful family style stood out as quite distinct from the others. Adolescent young men growing up within this parenting style spent more time with the peer group than other adolescents and they had a very negative attitude towards school as well as to the family. They were also more likely to feel peer pressure to drink and smoke and to regard theft and vandalism as justified in certain circumstances. Although they hung around with friends they did not regard themselves as easy to get along with and they were more likely to report psychological stress. This family type appeared to have a long-term impact. Two years later the levels of psychological stress were still raised among these young men and their general health was more likely to be assessed as poor.

The findings presented in this book reflect aspects of the interpretations of previous studies concerning home background such as Hendry *et al.*'s (1993) longitudinal investigation. What we have found here was that beyond social class differences, being looked after by adults who were *not* relatives; having parents or guardians who held low expectations of young people; and, for boys, having especially poor relationships with their father were significant social background factors in relation to the adolescent's disruptive behaviour.

Nevertheless, these ecological factors of psycho-social growth at the micro-system level, as Bronfenbrenner (1979) describes them, interact with an important social institution, namely schools (i.e. Bronfenbrenner's meso-system), in enabling young people's socialization towards adulthood to occur.

Uncertainty about occupational socialization and family breakdown are popularly cited as reasons for manifestations of disaffected youth. Yet it is difficult to quantify whether or not youth is more violent and rebellious than twenty, fifty or a hundred years ago. Davis (1990) argues that since the turn of the twentieth century adult society retains a 'public' image of the adolescent generation as rebellious, idle, sinful and delinquent!

As we argued in Chapter 1, the possibility that disaffection and delinquency in our society are in some measure the cost of certain kinds of social development. It has been argued that the predominant ethic of our society is acquisitiveness and desire for success. But not everyone can be rich or successful legitimately. Several writers have pointed out that the values underlying juvenile delinquency may be far less deviant than is commonly assumed. Other writers highlight adolescence itself as a problem rather than social disadvantage. Adolescents are, by their very nature, heavily influenced by peer group norms, prone to risk-taking and likely to be thrill-seeking. Boys are the biggest proportion of juvenile offenders and enter the justice system at an earlier age than girls. In 1961 the peak age for male offenders was 14 years. By the 1990s the peak age had increased to 18 years mainly because of changes in the system of juvenile justice. Yet if we are interested in ensuring young people's engagement with society, developing their skills of 'citizenship' and of empowering their legitimate self-agency, the school as a key social – and socializing – institution requires some 'fine-tuning' within the context of its wider community (i.e. Bronfenbrenner's eco-system and macro-system).

Young people in schools

As Jeffs (1994) points out British schools are 'depressing places' for those sympathetic to young people's rights. Moreover, it is claimed that it is the failure to treat young people as emerging adults that leads to the increasing number of truancies, expulsions and suspensions in schools as well as the breakdown of discipline. Truancy in schools, according to Demarco (1978), occurs because children are simply 'voting with their feet' about schools and what passes for education. This has been endorsed in Jeffs' (1994) book by his stressing that by far the most common cause for truancy is dissatisfaction with the content and quality of individual lessons. It has been claimed that denial of rights in education carries on despite legislation like the Children and Young People's Act of 1989 (Alderson, 1992) whose intention was to take into account the views of young people concerning their future well-being (Freeman, 1994). Some children are being denied their decision-making rights in developing policy-making in schools or in making representations to the body deciding whether or not they may be re-admitted to school in cases of expulsion (Franklin, 1994).

(a) Disruptive behaviour

Power *et al.* (1967) challenged the then conventional wisdom that family and social background were the principal influences on children's educational progress and on their social adjustment to school. Power's central question, and that of successive school researchers, was:

Does it matter which school a child or young person attends?

Rutter *et al.* (1979) found *no* relationship between pupil behaviour in school and the 'balance of intake' measured by academic ability band and parental occupation. On the other hand they found major differences between their twelve schools in scores on the pupil behaviour scale. Moreover,

the secondary schools with the worst behaviour in the classroom and on the playground were *not* necessarily those with the 'worst' intakes of difficult pupils at the age of ten years.

(p. 74)

A study of Inner London Junior Schools reached a similar but less clear-cut conclusion (Mortimore *et al.,* 1988). One reason for Mortimore's findings may simply be that:

nearly 30 per cent were noted as having shown some kind of behavioural problem during the first three years of junior school. Of these children, 13 per cent had behaviour problems in two or more years. However, only a very small minority were repeatedly assessed as disturbed in each of the three years (3 percent).

(p. 104)

In other words, children's behaviour changed from year to year with (for some) a change of class teacher. This implies that differences between teachers are substantially greater than between schools (Rabinowitz, 1981).

Aspects of the educational and social climate in the school and the classroom appear to constitute the principal influence on pupils' behaviour within the school itself and are of far greater importance than constitutional factors in the pupils themselves or social factors in their home backgrounds. High levels of minor disruptions are common but vary widely from school to school. Gray and Sime (1989) found only one per cent of teachers rated discipline problems in schools as 'very serious' and only fifteen per cent as 'serious'. Clearly, it is only a small minority of pupils whose behaviour in school causes concern.

Rutter *et al.* (1979) suggests the existence of substantial school effects; that there is '*something*' about certain schools in themselves which is associated with low rates of educational achievement and high rates of behavioural deviance amongst pupils. Rosser and Harré (1976) investigate school situations and find different accounts from the teachers' and pupils' perspective. What is important, they argue, is not what happened but what was understood, justified and conceived. Their revelations draw our attention to the orderliness of the social landscape viewed from the pupils' viewpoint. They discovered that pupils had their own complex rules by which they accounted for behaviour in school. Pupils justified actions according to two components:

- elaborate categorizations of occasions of offence;
- specific principles by which retribution for the offence was meted out.

There were a number of categories of offence:

- Teachers who were 'a load of rubbish'. These incorporated those staff perceived to be arrogant, 'distant', who saw a teaching job narrowly as purveyors of knowledge and nothing else, who dashed off immediately after school.
- Offences of 'anonymity'. Pupils complained of being depersonalized, of being treated contemptuously by teachers

who didn't even know their names. (Failure of headteachers in this respect were particularly despised.)

- 'Soft teachers'. One of the worst categories. Pupils felt particularly offended by weakness, felt let down in relation to expectations of strength in authority figures.
- 'Unfairness' — Sibling comparisons were highly offensive;
  - Position of pupil in power hierarchy (kids feeling 'put down' or 'picked on');
  - Unjust punishment/punishments unrelated to crime.

There were two main principles of retribution which explained, quite logically to the pupils, the sorts of response which such offences brought forth:

- Principles of reciprocity; where the pupils gave back what they got (insult for insult, 'hit for hit');
- Principles of equilibration; where pupils ignored teachers totally and withdrew into silence. This was used particularly when pupils felt 'put down' and was a means of restoring lost pride and dignity.

Rosser and Harré (1976) describe these as 'orderly and rule-bound' action sequences administered by pupils who view school as being essentially 'unserious', treating them in a depersonalized way (e.g. Hargreaves (1982) offers a similar account of how the 'hidden curriculum' creates opposition to school values and a counter-culture of dignity through such conflict).

What we have highlighted in relation to schools in this book leads to a number of 'policy and practice' proposals, supported by the research evidence already quoted in this section of the chapter. Looking first at the macro-system of the school, we would propose that schools need to ensure a more sympathetic and empathetic ethos. The findings of

Rutter *et al.* (1979), Mortimore *et al.* (1988) together with other texts on effective schools (e.g. Reid *et al.,* 1988) suggest the important elements which combine to develop the components of an 'empathetic' ethos. However, it is vital to reiterate that 'schools are different', hence no set formula can be offered beyond ensuring that the physical and social setting are pleasant; expectations are high; relationships between teachers and pupils are respectful, professional and warm; pupils are trusted and respected; they are given roles of responsibility and their academic and artistic work is on public display. Such contextual and social aspects appear to enhance young people's self-image and self-esteem, and in that connection our findings show that low self-esteem – in relation to 'social' self, 'academic' self and 'personal' self – is closely related to disruptive behaviour in both primary and secondary school sectors. The major influence on classroom motivation and behaviour of a very large majority of pupils appears to be the teacher: the dominant influence on their behaviour at school and outside the classroom appears to be the social ethos of the school.

Reflecting on the evidence of Rabinowitz (1981) and Gray and Sime (1989) that teachers' behaviours are central to the ways in which adolescent pupils respond to life in the classroom, and that a very small percentage of teachers consider there are serious discipline problems in schools, our findings reveal that pupils value teachers who give interesting lessons, have a pleasant, humorous manner in their relationships with pupils and can communicate effectively, can exercise good class control and show a genuine interest in pupils. At the classroom level teaching qualities remain much the same over time (see e.g. Hargreaves, 1982). It is also important to note that young people have a desire for rules within schools, but these need to be positive and relevant to adolescents' present lives and be in accord with their value-systems. Perhaps we should remember Franklin's (1994) 'message' that young people should be included in the negotiations and agreements surrounding decision-making which impinges on their daily lives.

(b) Exclusions

The criteria for school exclusion vary from school to school and relatively only small numbers of pupils are involved (Galloway *et al.,* 1982; Sanders, 1990). Galloway *et al.* (1985) found no association between the frequency of long-term or indefinite exclusion and aspects of social disadvantage from 36 secondary schools in one city. Schools serving the most socially disadvantaged parts of the city were neither more nor less likely to exclude large numbers of pupils than schools serving the most privileged areas. Nor was there any statistically significant relationship between exclusion rates and the large number of variables related to structural aspects of the school, such as size and age, or formal aspects of its organization, such as policy on ability groupings or the organization of pastoral care. McManus (1987) and McLean (1987) also found significant differences between schools in exclusion rates.

Much media attention has been drawn to the issue of exclusion of pupils from school over the past few years. Imich (1996) focused on findings accumulated over a five-year period. This evidence confirms that permanent exclusions from school have increased threefold in the period and that at present one pupil in five hundred is permanently excluded each year. The overwhelming majority of these pupils (85 per cent) are male, with a peak age for exclusion being 14 years. It appears that a small number of school are responsible for the majority of exclusions, and there is no relationship with the socio-economic status of the schools' catchment area. The most common reason for exclusion is general disruption and unacceptable behaviour, with physical abuse of staff accounting for only three per cent of all exclusions. Imich's most recent evidence suggests that the number of exclusions are continuing to rise. By secondary age, 'excluded' pupils are not as linguistically competent as their peers which can lead them to attempt the physical resolution of peer-group problems, rather than the use of less aggressive social skills techniques.

Most excluded pupils report difficulties in their school work as well as in pupil and teacher relationships. Such pupils had these difficulties at primary school, but felt they became more pronounced at secondary level. Interestingly, the pupils usually reported that they were not aware just how close they were to a permanent exclusion. This suggests a need for increased pupil involvement in their own behaviour management. The evidence presented argues that exclusion is strongly related to social processes within the school, and that these are *not necessarily* the same social processes as those associated with more general measures of disaffection or school disruption.

Imich's (1996) report on exclusions has provided a picture of the characteristics and qualities of these pupils; what we would wish to extract from our findings at this stage are the following two points. First, there is a 'blame culture' which is in operation where schools are perceived to be, and feel themselves to be, somehow 'at fault' when pupils are excluded. Secondly, and associated with the first point, the reasons for the processes and procedures leading up to exclusion are complex and multifaceted. We have shown the variations within and between schools over time, and it is clear that these difficulties are not simply school-based problems – though schools are the context in which they are acted out – and involve relational difficulties, and poor social skills, personality clashes, learning 'inconsistencies', low self-esteem, and possibly a range of background (social) variables.

Such findings raise the whole issue of how we can find new approaches to working with young people in a way that enables them to develop social skills within a metacognitive framework (see page 195).

By complete contrast to the picture of exclusion and of school behaviour in the case of juvenile delinquency, there *is* a very strong relationship with factors in the pupils' home backgrounds, particularly parental discord (e.g. West and Farrington, 1977). This does *not* mean, however, that all, or even most, young people from 'difficult' homes with low incomes are likely to be delinquents. As Galloway (1995) has noted, it does mean that the prevalence of these problems is greater in schools admitting large numbers of pupils from such homes: nevertheless schools can reduce the risk of the problem – or increase it. Pupils who are excluded from school constitute a high-risk group both for delinquency and for truancy (Galloway *et al*, 1982; Galloway and Barrett, 1984). While in Galloway's research most offences were committed *before* exclusion, common sense suggests that following exclusion pupils are likely to be at even greater risk of disruptive and delinquent behaviours.

The adolescent years are a period when great adjustments have to be made by young people to changes both within themselves and in society and in relation to the expectations which society places on them. Many young people make the transition to adulthood with relative ease but some are handicapped by economic and structural forces which make their passage to a worthwhile adult status very difficult. Others have the misfortune to have to cope with too many challenges to their self-esteem and identity at one time. For some young people in these positions antisocial behaviour or self-destructive behaviour can be the consequence of their need to find either status or solace. How can professionals in schools and community work assist young people's development?

New approaches to behaviour

Baron and Brown (1991), in America, argue that schools have neglected the metacognitive skills of decision-making, an area that some educators might call critical thinking. They propose a number of specific programmes for developing decision-making, an area that some educators might call critical thinking. They propose a number of specific programmes for developing decision-making into an important educational focus. For example, they outline a GOFER curriculum (i.e. Goals, Options, Facts, Effects and Review). Another decision-making process is GOOP (Goals, Options, Outcomes and Probabilities). These programmes attempt to provide pupils with training in critical thinking that allows them to simplify complex problems. Such metacognitive skills are too valuable to be reserved for the cognitive domain alone and we would want to suggest an extension of these ideas as a framework for considering not only the intellectual but also the emotional (i.e. 'feeling') and social components involved in the development of young people's abilities as they move towards the adult world. The individual adolescent's powers of reasoning need to be developed in relation to self, to others, to acquiring various social skills, to approaches to learning; and a metacognitive understanding of learning styles should be encouraged (e.g. Nisbet and Shucksmith, 1984). Young people need to be encouraged to understand cause, effect and consequences and to be helped to understand the social skills and strategies that lead to effective decision-making not only in academic work but in social contexts, too.

Hendry (1993) proposes a new emphasis on social education in schools – a new 3Rs for pupils to learn. These 3Rs should be called Reflection, Responsibility and Relationships.

(i) Reflection (or metacognitive skills)

The critical test of good learning is shown in the ability of the learner to demonstrate critical thought and to transfer knowledge or skills from the context in which they were first encountered to novel or problematic situations. Too much of what is learned at school cannot or is not used in the face of real-life dilemmas. Many skills, it is claimed, are too task-specific and they are not taught to young people with generalization in mind. Pupils are not taught to take over responsibility for monitoring the way in which skills are used or the context in which they are to be used and thus they have trouble applying them again on their own initiative. Nisbet and Shucksmith (1984) suggest a hierarchical model which distinguishes task-oriented and highly *specific skills* from *learning strategies* which represent super-ordinate skills, generalized procedures or sequences of activities with a common purpose. These elements are as necessary as the task-specifics and involve such strategies as planning, reviewing, self-monitoring, critical self-appraisal and so on. Many of these strategies are metacognitive in character, that is, they involve the learner in being aware of his or her own pattern and style of thinking and working, his or her own orientations to learning contexts, and awareness of alternative strategies, thus being placed in a position of choice within a framework of 'learning to learn'.

(ii) Responsibility

Responsibility essentially means an enhancement of the young person's self-agency. These qualities too demand the employment of metacognitive insight. The development of such skills and abilities point towards the young person's ability to control his or her own development – not only being influenced by events but also influencing these changes within one's own life spheres. Even outside the school setting, young people are often aware that they are denied a role in collaboration with adults in making decisions. A study of the benefits of youth work found that adolescents' perceptions of youth work settings, where professional leaders had the clear aim of encouraging young people to share and be involved in decision-making, were that they felt excluded from the process and in the main 'adults make the decisions' (Love and Hendry, 1994). Perhaps we should recognize more powerfully that the ways in which young people understand and perceive themselves and their own potential for self-agency in various social situations have a potent effect on their subsequent reaction to various life events.

(iii) Relationships

The third 'R' revolves around the necessity for the competent youngster to have an understanding of, and skills needed for, social relationships. In this way social roles are developed by young people in their relationships with adults and *conformist* youth are socialized in the image of their adult mentors. Involvement in adult-led organizations provides an opportunity for those adolescents who attend clubs to associate with adults beyond the family on a regular basis at the same time as pursuing more casual leisure interests that can continue to align themselves with their peers. In this way they have 'a foot in both camps', so to speak, and the opportunity to experience a wide range of social roles, while absorbing and accepting adult attitudes. But adolescents have a potentially wide network of social relations, and the strength of peer involvement in mid-adolescence is powerful. The lure of the peer group in terms of social behaviour is often irresistible, so while conformist youth may continue to be more attracted to adult organizations and influence this does not touch other adolescents. Without the influence of caring adults various deviant patterns can emerge, reflecting particular value systems, reinforced by peer relationships and images from adult society.

Case studies*

A number of schools have moved in the direction of developing such social and metacognitive skills in pupils in the context of school disruption. Two examples are presented to illustrate different successful approaches.

(a) At Forres Academy, a secondary school, the rules governing behaviour are devised by teachers after detailed discussion with their classes. The system then involves a series of warnings for pupils who break the agreed guidelines. After warnings they are sent to spend the rest of the lesson in Time Out, a classroom supervised full-time by a member of the teaching staff. Crucially, they carry on working but must complete a questionnaire which asks them to reflect on their misconduct and explain why they misbehaved. They then take the document home to complete a second section with a parent present. If they are referred to Time Out three times, the school calls a case conference, in which parents, teachers and the head produce a plan for action in consultation with the disruptive pupil. It is only after nine sessions in Time Out that the head teacher decides the pupil is a lost cause who deserves to be expelled.

The head teacher at Forres says established punishments used by many Scottish schools, including after-school detentions and punishment exercises such as lines, have failed. 'If punishment worked then schools wouldn't continue to have problems. Why not find a more sensible way out that is better for everybody's nerves, both pupil and teacher? The idea is that we can help the disruptive children rather than just giving them lines and forgetting about them.'

Forres Academy claims their approach has reduced confrontation between pupils and teachers, and encouraged pupils to tell the truth about misconduct because they have 'nothing to fear'.

---

* These two case studies were extracted from then current newspaper reports of the two schools.

(b) Brooke Weston City Technology College in Corby has no formal disciplinary procedures and no system of punishments. There is no staff room; teachers and students share territory, just as they queue up together for lunch. Every youngster has a personal tutor who must support him or her in a dispute. The working week of Brooke Weston's pupils is more than nine hours longer than the national average. At Brooke Weston there was a 98.25 per cent attendance rate in 1994–95. The head sets targets for teachers and pupils. At the beginning of each term the pupils are told what will be expected of them. Their progress is monitored. They are constantly encouraged to excel; asked what they want to do, and then told that they can do it if they try. In terms of exam results, Brooke Weston is already among the top 100 state schools, and unlike most of the rest, it is not selective. Nor is the intake excessively middle-class. Until recently, Corby was a steel town. It has deprived areas and tough council estates. The school's relations with parents are excellent; one reason why there are so few disciplinary problems. Not only are there regular parents' evenings: for one week a year all parents are allowed unlimited access to the school. They can arrive without notice in their own child's classroom, or in any other classroom.

All Brooke Weston's pupils spend their first two years in mixed-ability classes. Then they are setted in four groups: basic, standard, extended and advanced. They themselves have the final say over the set that they join, though they are normally happy to be guided by their teachers. So they proceed towards public examinations, and yet again, Brooke Weston has its own way of doing things. Pupils take GCSE when they are ready, not simply when they reach the appropriate chronological age!

These two case studies are illustrative of whole-school approaches, which we would endorse as ways in which pupil disaffection may be resolved, and which are practical ways of adapting the findings of our own studies into policy and practice.

Final comments

Claxton (1984) comments that for many pupils school does work – 'it meets their needs, feeds their interests, creates opportunities. For others school holds out rewards that they know they will not get and do not even want.' Yet they all need to find their place in society! If we wish to change 'school climate' and provide self and social management skills for young people we need to take real account of the ways in which they think about school and other organizations in our society. On the one hand we regard young people as representatives of a future generation which will direct and control numerous spheres of human activity in society. But on the other hand we make little attempt to seek their opinion in a way which would make a formative contribution to shaping their future schooling or community life. Yet, if we genuinely believe in their worth (to say nothing of the importance of their original thinking) this is precisely what we ought to be doing in order to convey the message that young people can exercise a positive influence over their own destiny. As long as we omit to ask them for their viewpoint we stand in danger of implying that their ideas are actually held in low regard, or are somehow 'flawed' or that 'we know best at all times and in all circumstances'.

A study by Branwhite (1988) shows that young people value incentives related to their personal school achievements and social behaviour. As evidence that they were Thatcher's heirs, incentives for good work was most often linked to tangible incentives, such as certificates, tokens, trophies, shields or badges, money or consumable elements such as sweets. In dealing with behaviour-related incentives the preference was for social outcomes, including being given 'free' time and receiving praise from teachers. Incentives are not the whole story, however, and young people indicated that empathy was the most useful type of personal support that teachers could lend to them. This quality of empathy which is most highly appreciated by pupils includes: setting a good example, being friendly, listening, staying calm, giving encouragement, using humour and dealing fairly with problems. We might consider a greater in-service programme for teachers and other professionals working with young people aimed at developing and enhancing such interpersonal skills in order to assist, in turn, young people's self and social development. Overall, we are proposing greater emphasis on behaviour management by both professionals and young people for the benefit of social institutions such as schools, and hopefully, if the metacognitive and social competences are properly developed young people may be empowered and enabled to find their place within society. The hope for our educational institutions is that they become catalysts of positive change towards the future by encouraging a wide range of abilities, self-appraisal, independence, social skills, achievements, diversity and 'political' awareness. Young people need to be helped to be successfully proactive in a wide range of social contexts and institutions.

The dynamics of disruptive behaviour

The three broad factors, which we have discussed in this book – school ethos, the pupil's social background and self-esteem – interrelate very strongly, but their impact on each individual pupil varies significantly, creating a rather unpredictable scenario in relation to which it can be very difficult to identify the key factors in school disruption. Earlier studies have concentrated on identifying single factors associated with pupil disruption, hoping to find the holy grail which would explain all possible situations. But each pupil with a record of school disruption has a unique case history so that the significance of the three main forces discussed in this book and a myriad of associated influences will all have made some impact on pupil behaviour over time. Consequently research in the 1960s which identified home circumstances as a key factor has some validity. Equally the later research in the 1970s and 1980s which suggested a link between pupil behaviour and the ethos of the school had some powerful supporting arguments. But these two themes are not mutually exclusive nor do they represent the whole picture – our own research shows that a pupil's self-concept is also very important. But again this does not provide a simple answer to what causes the complex problem of disruptive behaviour. The three factors interact dynamically with infinite variations of importance from pupil to pupil and across time.

How do we change disruptive behaviour?

It has been argued that many of the changes in society during the past two decades have been presented in the mass media as having made a significant contribution to the deteriorating standards of young people's behaviour. Changes in home and family circumstances are closely related to societal changes (e.g. Bronfenbrenner, 1979). A number of 'parenting skills' initiatives have attempted to achieve the goal of positively influencing young people's behaviour but with a spectacular lack of success in terms of long-term benefits for adolescents, and as Hendry *et al.* (1993) amongst others have shown, particular parenting styles do have long-term effects – either positively or adversely – on adolescents' behaviour. The conclusion has to be that the context which can most effectively assist in improving pupil behaviour is the school itself. This may not be a startling conclusion but it coincides with the views of Rutter *et al.* (1979) yet for very different reasons. As Ruddock *et al.* (1996) suggest:

> The culture of childhood and adolescence has been redefined (and not for the first time in social history) through the conditions of unemployment, single parenting, family breakdown, and poverty. *We need to try to understand where young people are*

coming from and how such understanding can help us with the task of school improvement.

(present authors' emphasis)

Understandably school is perceived as a key determinant in resolving increased disaffection and disruption among young people but often it is seen as virtually the only means of tackling this issue (HMCI, 1996). Policy changes, as we have outlined in previous chapters, provide a framework for developing strategies but they must be translated into practical and pragmatic processes and procedures to improve the nature, quality accessibility and range of school opportunities for young people nationally. The 'interactive triangle' of home – school – pupil, within the widest contexts of a collaborative community and democratic society (Bronfenbrenner, 1979), must be maintained if we are to enhance young people's psycho-social development towards competent citizenship capable of self-agency and enabled to be participating partners with their elders. Otherwise youth disruption and disaffection will remain.

Bibliography

Alderson, P (1992) Rights of children and young people. In Coote, R (Ed) *The Welfare of Citizens: Developing New Social Rights.* London: Rivers Oram.

Baron, J and Brown, R V (1991) *Teaching Decision Making to Adolescents.* New Jersey: Hillsdale: Erlbaum Associates.

Brake, M (1985) *Comparative Youth Culture: The Sociology of Youth Cultures and Youth Sub-Cultures in America, Britain and Canada.* London: Routledge.

Branwhite, T (1988) 'The pass survey: school-based preferences of 500+ adolescent consumers'. *Educational Studies* 14:2 (165–76).

Bronfenbrenner, U (1979) *The Ecology of Human Development*. Harvard: Harvard University Press.

Claxton, G (1984) *Live and Learn: An Introduction to the Psychology of Growth and Change in Everyday Life*. London: Harper and Row.

Davis, J (1990) *Youth and the Condition of Britain: Images of Adolescent Conflict*. London: Athlone Press.

Demarco, L (1978) *Obedience to Authority*. In Aikenhead, L (Ed) *Children's Rights – Extinction or Rebirth*. Glasgow: SCCL.

Durkheim, E. (1964) *The Division of Labour in Society*. Free Press.

Franklin, B (1994) The Case for Children's Rights: A Progress Report in Franklin, B (Ed) *The Handbook of Children's Rights Comparative Policy and Practice*. London: Routledge.

Freeman, M (1994) Children's Rights in a Land of Rites. In Franklin, B (Ed) *The Handbook of Children's Rights Comparative Policy and Practice*. London: Routledge.

Galloway, D (1995) 'Truancy, Delinquency and Disruption: Differential School Influences?' *British Psychological Society (Education Section) Review*, 19, 2, 49–53.

Galloway, D, Ball, T, Blomfield, D and Seyd, R (1982) *Schools and Disruptive Pupils*. London: Longman.

Galloway, D and Barrett, C (1984) 'Factors Associated with Suspension from New Zealand Secondary Schools'. *Educational Review*, 36: 277–85.

Galloway, D, Martin, R and Wilcox, B (1985) 'Persistent Absence from School and Exclusion from School: The Predictive Power of School and Community Variables'. *British Educational Research Journal*, 1,1: 51–61.

Gray, J and Sime, N (1989) 'Teachers and Discipline: A Report for the Committee of Enquiry into Discipline in Schools by Sheffield University, Part 1. Findings from the 'National Survey of Teachers in England and Wales'. In DES *Discipline in Schools*. (The Elton Report). London: HMSO.

Hargreaves, D H (1982) *The Challenge for the Comprehensive School.* London: Routledge and Kegan Paul.

HMCI (1996) *Exclusions from Secondary Schools 1995/6: A Report from the Office of Her Majesty's Chief Inspector of Schools – OFSTED.* The Stationery Office.

Hendry, L B (1993) Learning the new 3R's? Educating young people for modern society. *Aberdeen University Review,* 189, 33–51.

Hendry, L B, Shucksmith, J, Love, J and Glendinning, A (1993) *Young People's Leisure and Lifestyles.* London: Routledge.

Imich, A (1996) Exclusions from school. *The Psychologist,* 8, 7, 306.

Jeffs, T (1994) Children's Educational Rights in a New Era? In Franklin, B (Ed) *The Handbook of Children's Rights Comparative Policy and Practice.* London: Routledge.

Jones, G and Wallace, C (1992) *Youth, Family and Citizenship.* Milton Keynes: Open University Press.

Love, J G and Hendry, L B (1994) Youth workers and youth participants: Two perspectives of youth work? *Youth and Policy,* 46, 43–55.

Maffesoli, M (1996) *The Time of the Tribes.* London: Sage.

Matza, A D and Sykes, G (1961) 'Juvenile delinquency and subterranean values'. *American Social Review,* 26, 712–19.

Mortimore, P, Sammons, P, Stoll, L, Lewis, D and Ecob, R (1988) *School Matters: The Junior Years.* Wells: Open Books.

McLean, A (1987) 'After the Belt: School Processes in Low Exclusion Schools', *School Organization,* 7 (iii): 303–10.

McManus, M (1987) Suspension and Exclusion from High Schools: The Association with Catchment and School Variables. *School Organisation,* 7, (iii): 261–71.

Nisbet, J and Shucksmith, J (1984) *Learning Strategies.* London: Routledge and Kegan Paul.

Power, M J, Alderson, M R, Phillipson, C M, Schoenberg, E and Morris, J M (1967) 'Delinquent Schools'. *New Society,* 10: 19.10. 542–3.

Rabinowitz, A (1981) The Range of Solutions: A Critical Analysis. In Gillham, B (Ed.) *Problem Behaviour in the Secondary School: A Systems Approach.* Croom Helm.

Reid, K, Hopkins, D and Holly, P (1988) *Towards the Effective School.* Oxford: Blackwell.

Rosser, E and Harré, R (1976) The Meaning of Trouble. In Hammersley, M and Woods, P (Eds) *The Process of Schooling.* Routledge and Kegan Paul.

Ruddock, J, Chaplain, R and Wallace, G (1996) *School Improvement. What Can Pupils Tell Us?* David Fulton Publishers.

Rutter, M *et al.* (1979) Fifteen Thousand Hours: Secondary Schools and their Effects on Children. Open Books.

Sanders, D. (1990) The Class Struggle. Unpublished PhD Thesis.

West, D J and Farrington, D P (1977) *The Delinquent Way of Life.* Heinemann.

Appendix A   Causes of disruption

What are the causes of disruption?

This book looks at this question from the young people's perspective. How do they relate to their family? What do they like and dislike about their teachers? Are more young people disaffected today? The central themes of this book are underpinned by the answers young people gave to questionnaire or interview questions in a research project based on 3000 young people in a large Scottish city (Sanders, 1990). The main emphasis of the research was to focus attention on the views and perceptions of pupils, teachers, headteachers and parents.

Pupil perspectives

There were two approaches to the study of pupils' perspectives: first, a relatively large-scale survey of mainstream primary and secondary pupils; secondly a case study approach to ten pupils from special education or education otherwise. For the former, 1776 primary school pupils representing 49 schools and 1303 secondary pupils from eleven schools were surveyed by questionnaire. The primary pupils were all in their final year of primary education and the secondary phase pupils were 13+. In each school all pupils were on a 'standard' timetable prior to subject choices having impacted on their programme. This was deemed important as its effect would be to magnify and vary any influences on each pupil.

The ten pupils from the special sector had all been excluded from mainstream schools and received some or all of their secondary education in segregated special school provision. The questionnaire was completed by all pupils and additionally the ten 'special pupils' were interviewed. Two main functions of the questionnaire were: to obtain pupil views on several issues and to assess each individual's self-concept. Scores were then compared with teachers' views of their propensity for disruption and analysis undertaken to establish if any relationship existed between pupil self-concept and their propensity for disruption. Pupils were also asked about their families, their attitude to school, preferred attitudes of teachers and worst punishments. The questions were drawn from the pupil self-concept studies undertaken by Youngman (1979); 'The Young People's Leisure and Lifestyles Project' developed by Hendry *et al.* (1993); and new questions designed specifically to examine pupils' views on aspects of schooling. The amalgamated questionnaire was extensively tested prior to the main research programme being initiated. The results of the questionnaire were analysed by a range of statistical techniques mainly relating to SPSS (Statistical Package for the Social Sciences). The ten 'special' pupils were selected from four different types of alternative provision and they were interviewed within two weeks of leaving school. It was felt that the proximity of their school leaving date would help them to be more realistic and reflective of their school experiences. The interview was semi-structured with particular emphasis being placed on the pupil's family background, recollections of primary and secondary schools and their teachers, incidents leading up the exclusion and their view of the quality of alternative provision. Additionally, the pupils were asked about their interests, peer and friendship groups and their plans and aspirations for the future.

Teacher and headteacher perspectives

As an integral part of the Scottish study and as another element of the research programme, pupils' primary and secondary teachers were asked to categorize levels and frequency of misbehaviour of the pupils whom they taught. These were cross-referenced with the views of the headteacher and school adviser, and the results used to give indication of pupil propensity for disruption. Separately for two clusters of schools a scale of pupil misbehaviour was calculated for each class and the 'scores' were used to establish an index of misbehaviour for each school. Additionally the views of teachers and headteachers were sought in relation to the changing standards of behaviour through time. The survey of headteachers was conducted separately and they were asked to give views on:

- the most common types of disruption
- the most difficult types of disruption
- the most effective sanctions
- recommendations to reduce the impact of disruption in schools.

For primary schools, which have a more distinct catchment area, the results in relation to the above were correlated against the type of housing, the size of the school and the style of the school.

Parental perspective

It was evident form the responses of headteachers and teachers that they believed effective behavioural management of disaffected adolescents required involvement of parents. Two avenues of research were explored in relation to the quality of liaison and communication between school staff and parents.

The school prospectus is a document required by law and widely circulated to parents. The first area of study related to the school prospectus and specifically its messages about discipline and sanctions. The second study centred on personal liaison between school staff and parents. There are several times when there is a need for very active liaison. Induction into a new school is an obvious example, as is the time of course selection prior to selecting subjects for the 16+ examination. To consider the parental perspective on the quality of school liaison at such times, sample populations of parents from two secondary schools and their feeder primary schools from contrasting areas socio-economically were surveyed by questionnaire. Parents of pupils who were close to completing their first year in primary or secondary school were approached for their views. Similarly the views of parents of pupils in their final year at primary school and those of pupils at 14+ who had already made subject choices were contacted. These particular cohorts were selected because for each group significant liaison between home and school would have recently been undertaken. Therefore parents should be in a good position to comment on the quality of relationship established between home and school and to establish a parental perspective on the quality of school behavioural policies in theory and practice. In total 401 parents of primary-age pupils and 323 parents of secondary school pupils were sampled.

Concluding comments

Thus the findings and ideas discussed in this book have been underpinned by an extensive research programme. Additionally, in writing this book the authors draw from a range of teaching, administrative and research experience related to the needs of and provision for disaffected young people.

Appendix B   Extracts from the pupil questionnaire

B1: Family Life Scale.

Items	Family Life Scale
1.	Get on well with mother/step-mother
2.	Get on well with father/step-father
3.	Father/step-father is too strict
4.	Mother/step-mother is too strict
5.	Parent/s want to know where go in evening
6.	Allowed to bring friends home
7.	What kids do outside the home is their own business
8.	Kids get into trouble for thrills
9.	Parent/s are proud of me
10.	Often quarrel with brother/sister
11.	Parent/s help with schoolwork

B2: Perception – Self, School and Teacher Scales.

Items	Perception – Self, School and Teacher Scales
1.	Lessons are interesting
2.	Enjoy doing homework
3.	Need rules
4.	Behave well
5.	Parents sort the teachers out
6.	School is boring
7.	Obeying rules is for the soft
8.	Wearing uniform is good
9.	Difficult to control temper
10.	Teachers are interested
11.	Told off when deserved
12.	School is great
13.	Rules cause trouble
14.	Truant
15.	Children behave well
16.	I destroy others' belongings
17.	Teachers pick on me
18.	Teachers are allright
19.	I like fighting
20.	I swear at teachers
21.	Teachers are too strict
22.	I hate this school
23.	I always tell the truth
24.	I do what the teacher tells me
25.	Wish gone to different school

B3: Self-concept – Social, Personal and Academic Scales.

Items	Self concept – Social, Personal and Academic Scales
1.	I forget to do things
2.	It's no use relying on me
3.	I get on with other children
4.	Other children like playing with me
5.	I don't understand class work
6.	I am popular
7.	I have lots of friends
8.	People are disappointed with me
9.	I wish teachers would explain things better
10.	Other children like working with me
11.	It's hard to be me
12.	I can generally work things out for myself
13.	I am often chosen as leader
14.	I have hardly any friends
15.	I am good at most things
16.	School work is easy
17.	Other children don't notice me
18.	Teachers think I'm good
19.	Other children pick on me

Appendix C Relationship of summary scores with behaviour categories by chi-square test

SUMMARY SCORES	GENERALLY WELL-BEHAVED PUPILS				POTENTIAL FOR SERIOUS DISRUPTION			
	PRIMARY		SECONDARY		PRIMARY		SECONDARY	
	MALE	FEMALE	MALE	FEMALE	MALE	FEMALE	MALE	FEMALE
QUESTION 8 - FAMILY	.000	0.5227	.0008	0.8599	0.0019	0.5839	0.0109	0.7006
QUESTION 13 - TYPE 1 (SELF)	.0000	0.0006	.0000	0.0006	0.0000	0.0000	0.0000	0.0013
- TYPE 2 (SCHOOL)	.0000	0.3076	.0000	0.2801	0.0028	0.0391	0.0004	0.1248
- TYPE 3 (TEACHER)	.0000	0.0001	.0000	0.0697	0.0000	0.0000	0.0000	0.3987
QUESTION15 - SELF-CONCEPT (SOCIAL)	.0002	0.0386	.0268	0.5273	0.0001	0.0011	0.0061	0.5572
(PERSONAL)	.0000	0.0003	.0000	0.0069	0.0001	0.0000	0.0000	0.0026
(ACADEMIC)	.0001	0.0938	.0000	0.7381	0.0050	0.0009	0.0000	0.5699

Appendix D Relationship of various parameters with pupil potential for disruption

Testing the relationship between pupil's potential for serious disruption and:

1. Father's occupation – question 5
2. Family circumstances – question 8
3. Pre-school arrangements – questions 9, 10 and 11
4. Pupil perception – question 13, and
5. Pupil self-concept – question 15.

Item	Primary		Secondary	
5. Father's occupation	**0.0002**	0.3637	**0.0001**	0.3246
8a. Get on well with mother/stepmother	0.1147	1	1	0.206
8b. Get on well with father/stepfather	**0.0151**	0.1902	**0.0446**	0.6998
8c. Father is too strict	0.8342	0.2224	**0.0092**	1
8d. Mother is too strict	0.7686	0.1285	0.2851	1
8e. Parents want to know where at night	**0.036**	0.0905	**0.0026**	0.8007
8f. Allowed to bring friends home	0.3213	1	0.2067	0.8007
8g. What kids do outside is own business	0.1267	0.4303	0.7438	1

Item	Primary		Secondary	
8h. Kids get into trouble for thrills	0.4281	0.412	0.5295	1
8i. Parents are proud of me	**0.0101**	0.4889	**0.0001**	**0.0227**
8j. Often quarrel with brother/sister	0.6949	0.3089	1	0.085
8k. Parents help with school work	0.2432	0.6722	**0.0364**	1
9. Looked after by non-relative	**0.0219**	0.1493	**0.0013**	0.5243
10. Pre-school play-group/nursery/both	**0.0113**	0.1154	0.0994	0.7354
11. Attended more than 1 primary school	0.0615	0.0547	**0.0016**	**0.0401**
12. Other primary in Aberdeen	0.5663	0.6791	0.1848	1
13a. Lessons are interesting	0.812	0.9504	0.255	0.1515
13b. Enjoy doing homework	0.7596	1	0.2186	0.3776
13c. Need rules	0.0577	1	**0.0032**	0.6926
13d. Behave well	0	0	0	0
13e. Parents sort the teachers out	0.2583	0.5033	0.3912	0.5562
13f. School is boring	0.1732	0.7804	0.0006	0.2303
13g. Obeying rules is for the soft	0,0013	0.8788	0.2874	0.9513
13h. Wearing uniform is good	0.9508	0.2765	0.1908	0.4935

Item	Primary		Secondary	
13i. Difficult to control temper	0	**0.0001**	0.1509	**0.0025**
13j. Teachers are interested	0.0103	**0.0021**	0.1744	-.1353
13k. Told off when deserved	0.6242	0	**0.043**	0.7444
13l. School is great	0.2785	0.6634	0.9726	0.2394
13m. Rules cause trouble	**0.0087**	1	**0.0005**	0.4808
13n. Truant	0.3586	0	0	0.3741
13o. Children behave well	0.0973	**0.0488**	0.1943	0.3108
13p. I destroy others' belongings	0.0763	0.5209	0.332	1
13q. Teachers pick on me	**0.0004**	**0**	**0**	**0.0117**
13r. Teachers are all right	0.1281	**0.0006**	**0.0002**	0.8183
13s. I like fighting	**0.0005**	**0.0001**	**0**	**0.0086**
13t. I swear at teachers	0	**0**	0.2105	1
13u. Teachers are too strict	**0.0034**	0.0572	**0.0255**	0,6014
13v. I hate this school	**0.0021**	0.626	**0.0009**	0.9125
13w. I always tell the truth	0.2395	0.6632	**0.041**	0.6057
13x. I do what the teacher tells me	**0**	**0**	**0**	0.1872
13y. Wish gone to different school	0.3061	0.3955	0.4206	0.3965
15a. I forget to do things	**0.0041**	0.2658	0	1
15b. It's no use relying on me	0.1346	**0.047**	0.5224	1
15c. Get on with other children	0.2597	**0**	**0.0101**	0.8814
15d. Children like playing with me	0.2926	0.1056	0.0655	0.7214

Item	Primary		Secondary	
15e. Don't understand classwork	**0.0117**	**0.0012**	**0.0447**	**0.0101**
15f. I am popular	0.2521	0.1457	0.41	0.8931
15g. Have lots of friends	**0.0455**	**0.0131**	**0.0092**	1
15h. People are disappointed with me	0	0	**0.0002**	0.1221
15i. Wish teacher explain things better	0.0611	0.2995	0.1569	0.2972
15j. Children like working with me	0.1167	**0.0005**	**0.0028**	1
15k. Hard to be me	0.2044	**0.004**	**0.001**	1
15l. Generally work things out myself	**0.036**	**0.0433**	**0.0035**	0.9659
15m. Often chosen as leader	**0.0004**	0.6366	0.0989	0.1037
15n. Hardly any friends	**0.0388**	0	0.0528	0.0831
15o. Good at most things	0.7085	0.2644	0.1398	0.6753
15p. School work is easy	1	0.1128	0.3722	0.9432
15q. Children don't notice me	0.5198	**0.0276**	0.1991	0.152
15r. Teacher thinks I am good	**0.015**	**0**	**0**	0.1021
15s. Children pick on me	0.9151	**0.0001**	**0.0063**	1

Appendix E Primary and secondary indices of misbehaviour

APPENDIX E PRIMARY AND SECONDARY INDICES OF MISBEHAVIOUR

MEAN INDICES	MACGILL(1)	MACGILL(2)	MACGILL(3)	MACGILL(4)	VERNALL(1)	VERNALL(2)	VERNALL(3)
BOYS	5.4	4.9	3.9	4.3	7.45	5.1	4.2
GIRLS	3.5	3.5	2.4	3.5	4.9	4.5	2.8
SCHOOL MEAN	4.3	4.2	3.2	4	6.1	4.7	3.5

SECONDARY SCHOOL RESPONSES TO INDICES OF MISBEHAVIOUR

	MACGILL			VERNALL		
	BOYS	GIRLS	MEAN	BOYS	GIRLS	MEAN
S1	2.9	2.2	2.6	4	2.6	3.2
S2	4.3	2.9	3.7	5.5	3	4.2
S3	3.9	2.3	2.5	5.6	3	4.2
S4	2.9	2.8	2.5	5.4	3.6	5.2
S5/6	1.7	1.2	1.6	3.2	2.2	2.8
TOTAL			12.9			19.6

Index